MW00563280

Growing Geraniums and Pelargoniums

Jean Llewellyn, Betty Hudson
and Gordon C. Morrison

Kangaroo Press

INTRODUCTION

The purpose of any introduction to a book is to give the prospective reader some idea of the aims and objects of the authors and why this book should be of interest and value.

Primarily it is written by Australians for conditions existing in Australia and for plants available in this country. However, the information contained herein is equally useful for growers in other countries, particularly those in temperate climates.

The authors have tried to ensure the accuracy of the terminology and nomenclature, an approach of major importance to all keen gardeners and horticulturists.

The presentation is such as to introduce the reader to the Geranium Family and explain how to identify and classify the most popular members of the family. This is a subject not well known to the gardening public or the nursery trade and is essential reading for the proper understanding of all that follows.

Growing procedures constitute a major part of the book, everything from buying the plants to their care in health and sickness. Finally the book lists recommended plants of both species and cultivars with a description of each and in some cases a photograph. The appendices provide both a word and pictorial description of some of the terms used.

There appears to be a significant need for a book which provides both a theoretical and practical guide to those interested in cultivating this family of plants; not only the gardener but the nurseryman and student of horticulture. By stating a little of the reasoning behind the recommendations made it allows the reader to use discretion and vary these to suit his needs.

It is the intention and hope of the authors that the chapters of this book will stimulate more interest in the Geranium Family and provide lots of help and ideas on the culture of a popular plant.

ACKNOWLEDGMENTS

We acknowledge the following for the use of their colour transparencies: C.E. Blackman, K. Bracher, Jeremy Bruhl, V.M. Butters, M.F. Edwards, R.E. Holborow, H.A. Llewellyn, G. Morf, G.C. Morrison, H.G. Wright, L.C. Yelds.

The line drawings are by Betty Hudson.

We are grateful to Macmillan, Melbourne, for permission to quote from *The Great Gardens of Australia* by Howard Tanner and Jane Begg and to Ure Smith for the quote from *Notes and Sketches of New South Wales during a residence in that Colony from 1839 to 1844* by Mrs Charles Meredith.

Kangaroo Press
3 Whitehall Road, Kenthurst 2154
Typeset by G.T. Setters Pty Limited
Printed in Hong Kong by Colorcraft Ltd

CONTENTS

Typical "Five Fingered" Pelargonium

1. BACKGROUND TO A FAMILY

An interesting feature of the times is the increasing interest in family backgrounds, the origin of the family name, its change over the years and in many cases its wide distribution.

As with people so it is with plant families. Today's gardeners are taking a closer look at the ancestry of the plants they grow and finding it a rewarding experience. The background of a plant family or even a group within that family can give many clues as to that plant's particular needs, its attributes and sometimes its failure in a given environment.

This book deals with the plant family GERANIACEAE. A large family embracing plants from many different countries of the world, having varying growth habits, flower shape, leaf texture, perfume and ornamentation. Commonly known as the geranium family it includes plants which grow in arid regions, others on mountains covered in snow for many months of the year. One, an endangered species, *Geranium arboreum* grows on the slopes of a crater in tropical Hawaii.

The name "geranium" whether correctly or incorrectly used has, over the years, come to mean many things to many people. For some it will recall childhood memories, others the drought-like conditions of Henry Lawson's *Water them Geraniums*; it may bring to mind pictures of radiant colour or produce an awareness of an elusive but pervading perfume.

Is it any wonder then, that a family of such wide distribution and infinite variation, should have such a popular appeal?

The origins of many long-cultivated plants are still obscure, and so it is with Geraniaceae. The first mention is in *Materia Medica*, a book of herbal remedies, written by Dioscorides about AD 50. The name used by Dioscorides was *Geranion* from the Greek *geranos*, a crane, referring to the similarity of the long-beaked fruit (seed capsule) to the bill of the crane.

Botanical Latin is an international language used by botanists for naming and describing plants, and names given are usually descriptive of some feature of the plant or named after the person who first discovered such plant. Botanical nomenclature requires that scientific plant names be in Latin form, or at least treated as such, even if derived from other languages, therefore *Geranion*—GERANIACEAE.

Whilst the origin of the family is obscure, we do know that early explorers and botanists discovered species of plants which showed characteristics sufficiently similar to be grouped into one large plant family, despite wide differences in distribution, appearance and growth habits. The characteristic which distinguishes this family from all others is the long-beaked fruit (seed capsule) resembling the bill of the crane.

The early discoveries in Europe and Asia were of plants, mostly perennial, having tufted foliage forming neat clumps or mats, with leaves variously lobed or dissected. Flowers, five petalled, regular in form (actinomorphic) and ranging in colour from white, through pink to blue, mauve and even magenta. Two of the earliest to be recorded were *Geranium macrorrhizum* (1576) and *Geranium striatum* (1629). Both were descriptive names, *macrorrhizum*—large rooted; *striatum*—streaked. Both these species were found in Southern Europe, the former having large roots, growth to approximately 28 cm (11") with five lobed leaves and flowers of dark red or bright purple; the latter a somewhat loose plant with handsomely cut basal leaves and a long succession of pale pink flowers streaked or pencilled with veins of brownish-red.

In ensuing years many more discoveries were made, and could possibly still be made, to add to the present listing of about 250 of these interesting *Geranium* species.

In another part of the world explorers and botanists were discovering other plants. Plants dissimilar in growth, leaf form and flower shape, and yet, still having the same distinctive long-beaked fruit resembling the bill of the crane. Some of these interesting discoveries had spine-like stipules, others large tuberous roots to conserve moisture in this harsh, dry land, and yet others with upright growth and flowers of bright scarlet or vivid purple.

With the formation of the Dutch East Indies Company in the 1600's many voyages were made between Europe, India and the East Indies travelling round the Cape of Good Hope, which was, at that time, in the control of the Dutch. The Cape became an important stop on this route for trading vessels, and the botanists and explorers fascinated by the discovery of these unusual plants, soon became aware of their potential.

In 1609 a Dutch Governor of the Cape sent to Holland a plant, the leaves of which were marked in the shape of a horseshoe. Plants of this type were later to become one of the parents of the zonal pelargonium of today.

One of the first of these South African discoveries to reach England, and to flower there, was recorded as having the name *Geranium indicum odoratum*. Seen flowering in the garden of John Tradescant in July 1632, it was described as having flowers of a dull yellowish-green with brownish-purple marks on each petal, and heavily perfumed at night. The leaves, finely divided, drooping to the ground and resembling those of the carrot. The root system a large subterranean tuber and tuberous roots. The name later applied to that plant was *Pelargonium triste* (tristis: sad, dull coloured).

These early discoveries in the Southern Hemisphere excited the botanists and explorers of the time and soon many more of these species were transported to other lands. Plants with tall, shrubby foliage and bright purple flowers to influence the ancestry of the regal pelargonium, others with trailing, sprawling, sometimes climbing habit, having succulent leaves shaped like a shield, were destined to become the parents of the ivy-leaved pelargonium.

The identification of these plants, as with the discoveries in Europe and Asia, was by the long-beaked fruit and so the botanists of the day classified them all as geraniums. It was not until 1789 that a French botanist, Charles Louis L'Heritier designated them as belonging to the genus *Pelargonium*. It may well be that the earlier classification under *Geranium* is the main contributing factor in the confusion of names within the family GERANIACEAE, and which exists even today. The early designation of *Geranium zonale* for what was subsequently designated as *Pelargonium zonale* may well account for the common usage terminology of "geranium" for the zonal pelargonium.

During the ensuing years more species were found in many areas of the world to join the growing collection of plants, all with the same distinctive long-beaked fruit. It is not surprising then, that botanists and writers began recording, describing and illustrating these plants. Beautifully illustrated books such as *Hortus Elthamensis*, 1732; *Rariorum*

Africanarum Plantarum, 1738; and *Geraniologia, sue Erodii, Pelargonii, Geranii, Monsoniae et Grieli Historia iconibus illustrata*, 1792, were published and eagerly sought after.

Gardeners and nurserymen of the time realizing the potential of these plants began hybridizing and soon produced new plants, some with flower forms and colours that had not been seen before, not even imagined, others with leaves having ornamentation of the most vivid hues. Such plants quickly became fashionable and the glasshouses and conservatories of Victorian times were soon filled with these highly coloured and decorative pelargoniums. Exhibitions were held and high commendations given for new and worthwhile introductions. Not only in England, but in Europe also, work on these species was being done, and the *Pelargonium*, in all its new found beauty, became the popular plant of the day.

On 26th August 1768 a ship sailed from England, bringing Captain James Cook, Joseph Banks and his assistant, a famous botanist named Dr Solander. The Endeavour arrived at a bay, in the great South Land, and here anchor was dropped on the morning of 29th April, 1770. The bay was named Stingray Bay by Captain Cook, but was later changed to Botany Bay at the request of Joseph Banks.

It was early in May, during the stay of the Endeavour in this bay, that Joseph Banks and Dr Solander found the first geraniums in this new land. Plants were collected of specimens having the distinctive long-beaked fruit and so were classed as geraniums. They were subsequently recorded as *Geranium pilosum* (later to be known as *Geranium solanderi*) and *Geranium australe* (later *Pelargonium australe* **Plate 2**).

In later years other specimens within GERANIACEAE were found, some indigenous, others introduced and naturalized. There are presently recorded ten *Geranium*, two *Erodium* and seven *Pelargonium* indigenous species in Australia.

There is widespread conjecture about the introduction and subsequent naturalization of such South African species as *Pelargonium capitatum*, in this country. There are two popular theories. One that trading vessels travelling via the Cape of Good Hope off-loaded their cattle to graze at the Cape, whilst grazing seeds attached to the coats of the animals and were later shed on the virgin soil of this new country. The other that ships stopping at the Cape used sand from the area for ballast before making the crossing of the Indian Ocean. Many ships were wrecked in those early days and the supposition is that the sand washed ashore and with it some of the seeds which, when reaching dry land grew and flourished. Either seems plausible for *Pelargonium capitatum* had, prior to reclamation work, naturalized itself and flourished along the shores of Botany Bay and can still be found growing profusely on the Kurnell peninsula.

With the founding of the Colony in 1788, and the continuing arrival of many settlers it was only natural that the plants they grew and loved in their home country should be transplanted. Many brought plants or seeds with them and it was not long before Sydney town blossomed with "geraniums". The decorative charm of the common plantings of some of the earliest gardens, moved Captain Kent to write: 'Geraniums flourish in such abundance, that in various parts of the settlement they are made into hedges, and are so thick as to be impenetrable; they are always in leaf and flower, and emit an odour of the most fragrant nature, perfuming the surrounding atmosphere'.

In 1826 there arrived in Sydney a nurseryman from Hackney, near London, and named Thomas Shepherd. Governor Darling, perceiving the need for a nursery in this new colony, made a grant of 28½ acres of land available in the vicinity of Shepherd Street, Darlington, for Shepherd to establish an area for growing vegetables and fruit trees. This Shepherd did, and the nursery became known as the Darling Nursery. Thomas Shepherd died in 1835 but the nursery continued on and in later years catalogues of this nursery listed many ornamentals, including pelargoniums.

In those early days "geraniums" were found in many gardens, were used to adorn gravestones of loved ones, and even taken by the families as they moved further out to Parramatta and beyond. Mrs Charles Meredith writing in her *Notes and Sketches of New South Wales during a residence in that Colony from 1839 to 1844* says: 'Geraniums thrive and grow rapidly, but I did not see any good ones; none that I would have thought worth cultivating in England. A Horticultural Society has now been established some years and will doubtless be the means of much improvement'.

In the following years nurseries were established in other states as well as New South Wales and many new plants were imported from England and Europe. Some hybridization was done locally and names such as 'Hobart Town', 'Maid of Tasmania' and 'Mayor of Melbourne' bore testimony to their Australian origin.

Back in the old world new books were being published, hand illustrated in colour and portraying the beautiful new introductions of such hybridizers as Grieve, Catleugh, Gaines and others. Rare these days, considered collectors pieces, such books as *Geraniaceae*, 1820–26; *Flore des Serres et des Jardins de L'Europe*, 1847 and *Les Geraniums*, 1897 are worth seeking in the libraries of the world.

The pelargonium craze continued until the First World War. During the post war period a few collections were maintained by keen gardeners, here and overseas, but it was not until after World War II that interest was again renewed. Enthusiasm once more developed and hybridizers, nurserymen and writers, again extolled the virtues of the *Pelargonium*. Societies specializing in these plants were formed and are now popular meeting places for enthusiasts in many countries of the world (Appendix 2).

New and distinct plants were, and are still being produced in many countries, and no less so than here in Australia. Popular books dealing with the knowledge and culture of the geranium family in all its many and varied forms, were, and are still being published. This book is added to the list.

The interest in the "geranium" is as strong today as it was in the 1800's. The colourful pelargoniums are being used in modern landscaping, the old world charm of the scented leaved group is being revived, and an awakening interest in the more unusual and less well-known species ensures the geranium family a promising future.

Australian gardeners have again become aware of the adaptability and unique character that various members of this family can contribute to their gardens.

2. IDENTIFICATION & CLASSIFICATION

The previous chapter dealt briefly with the background of the geranium family, with its many differing plant forms and yet with one distinguishing feature, the long-beaked fruit. How, because of the identification of this characteristic all these varying plant forms were grouped together into one large plant family and classified as GERANIACEAE (*geranos:* a crane).

This chapter aims to explain, in simple terms, the reason and usefulness of the classification and naming of plants (plant taxonomy) within that family.

The plant family to which this book relates is a large one. Whilst its origin is obscure it is known that early botanists identified within the family, plants which had other common characteristics and which warranted further classification within the family. The family was subsequently sub-divided into eleven genera (genus: *sing.* a group of plants having common structural characteristics differing from other groups within the family).

In recent years the family GERANIACEAE has been revised and such eminent botanists as Hutchinson (1969), Dr J.J.A. van der Walt (1977) and others, hold that this family should now be classified as having only five genera: *Sarcocaulon, Monsonia, Erodium, Geranium* and *Pelargonium.*

Sarcocaulon (*sarco*, fleshy; *caulon*, stem)

A group of plants restricted to Southern Africa and comprising about fifteen species. (Species: a botanical classification subordinate to that of genus and comprising a group of plants that is recognized as existing in nature and having the same constant and distinct characters.) It should be noted that the word species is used in both the singular and plural form, and should not be confused with the term specie: coin, as opposed to paper money.

The plants within genus *Sarcocaulon* are described as being sub-shrubs with rigid spreading branches, fleshy stems with spines (hardened leaf stalks) and small, sometimes tufted, leaves. *Flowers are regular in shape* (actinomorphic) *and have fifteen fertile stamens.* The colours range through creamy-white, pink, purple to red. They grow in arid regions and are known in their native land as "Bushman's Candles" because of the layer of resin on the stem which burns when lit. Some of the species recorded are *Sarcocaulon crassicaule, Sarcocaulon multifidum* and *Sarcocaulon mossamedense.* Few, if any, are available in Australia, being mainly found in cacti and succulent collections.

Monsonia (named in honour of Lady Anne Monson, a lady of considerable botanical knowledge and a correspondent of Linnaeus).

This genus consists of plants widely distributed throughout the African continent and a few in India. It is considered that of the 40 species recorded there are about 30 distributed throughout South Africa.

Described as bushy branched herbs or subshrubs, some annuals, others perennials. With varying leaf shapes, some stipulate, others finely cut, they have *flowers regular in shape and with fifteen fertile stamens.* Colours range from white, purple, and white to claret sometimes streaked or blotched. Some of the species recorded include *Monsonia speciosa, Monsonia ovata,* and *Monsonia biflora.* Few, if any, grown in Australia.

The remaining three genera, *Erodium, Geranium* and *Pelargonium* are all represented in Australia and are grown by many keen "geranium" enthusiasts.

Each of these genera, as well as having specific features which assist in their botanical classification, have one distinctive characteristic which makes for easy identification by the home gardener and this is the technique which each group uses to disperse the ripe seed.

In *Erodium* the fruit, when ripe, splits open into single seeded parts, each having its own spirally twisted or corkscrew-type tail. This spirally twisted tail thrusts the seed from the plant, which, on reaching the ground, is twisted into the soil. This action is brought about by the tail of the seed lengthening and recoiling as it is affected by atmospheric changes (**Plate 3**).

The other more popular genera *Geranium* and *Pelargonium* are still widely confused, possibly owing to the early classification of both under *Geranium*. However the seed dispersal technique of these two makes it an easy task for the home gardener to identify to which each belongs.

In *Geranium* the fruit, when ripe, splits open into single seeded parts with a catapult-like action twisting outwards and upwards. At the same time the case covering the tiny seed opens and flings the seed to the ground (**Plate 5**).

In *Pelargonium*, on the other hand, the fruit when ripe, splits open into single seeded parts, each having its own almost invisible spiral in front of a soft feathery end to the tail. The tiny spiral coils in dry weather thus separating the seed from the fruit, the feathery end to the tail assisting the seed to be borne away on the wind (**Plate 1**).

With these characteristics in mind it should now be easy for the home gardener to relate to the three genera, *Erodium*, *Geranium* and *Pelargonium* more fully described below.

Erodium (*Erodios,* a heron) "Heron's bill"

A group of plants mostly distributed throughout the Mediterranean region, with a few in Africa and Australia. Comprising about 60 species, they are classed as herbs and sub-shrubs, some annual and others perennial. *Flowers are regular and have ten stamens, five of which are fertile.* Their colours range from white, pink, sulphur-yellow, blue, to violet and purplish-red.

Erodiums are plants which enjoy sunny, well-drained positions and deep soil, ideal for rock gardens with their varying leaf shapes, growth habits and flower forms.

Many species have been introduced over the years and some of the more commonly grown ones are *Erodium hymenodes, Erodium gruinum* and *Erodium chamaedryoides*, (Syn. *Erodium reichardii*). An Australian species, *Erodium crinitum* with its small, intense blue flowers, showing the yellow anthers, is considered a weed and only good as fodder for animals. That is, of course, a matter of opinion!

Geranium (*Geranos,* a crane) "Crane's bill"

A genus of about 250 species of herbs, rarely sub-shrubs, mostly perennial, some annual, and distributed throughout the temperate regions of the world and to a large extent, the Northern Hemisphere. Some are found in South Africa, America, Australia and New Zealand.

Flowers are regular and with ten fertile stamens. The flower colour range is through white, pink, blue, purple to magenta. Flowers are produced in profusion during spring and summer. Leaves are variously cut and lobed and in some species the leaf colour changes to bright red in the autumn under dry conditions as does "Herb Robert" *Geranium robertianum*. The true *Geranium* is an adaptable plant for the rock garden and will grow in almost any soil but preferring a well drained one. Some species seed freely, particularly the annual types, others are best propagated by division when they die down for the winter. They should not be confused with the plants commonly and incorrectly called "geraniums" which do, in fact, belong to the Genus *Pelargonium* (which see). There are ten indigenous *Geranium* species in Australia, all others being introduced. Some of the more popularly grown ones being *Geranium robertianum, Geranium sanguineum* and *Geranium nepalense*.

Pelargonium (*Pelargos,* a stork) "Stork's bill"

Genus *Pelargonium* comprises about 200 species, the majority of which occur in South Africa, with a few in Tropical Africa, Syria, Australia and some islands in the Indian Ocean.

Described as being shrubby, somewhat succulent, erect or trailing, with varying leaf forms, many of which are scented. Flower colours range through white, pink, scarlet, purple and with some species shading to yellow and blue.

Flowers are irregular (zygomorphic) *having a nectar bearing tube and ten stamens, with not more than seven stamens being fertile.* It is here that the difference is noted: flowers are irregular, having a nectar bearing tube. The irregularity of the flowers and the nectar tube are two characteristics which make this group of plants distinct from those of genus *Geranium*, and which were responsible for the re-classification from genus *Geranium* to genus *Pelargonium* in 1789.

For the average gardener the nectar tube and the irregular shaped flowers are not easy to identify in the modern cultivar (cultivar—derived from *cul*tivated *var*iety). Whilst all other genera in GERANIACEAE are made up, almost entirely, of species (some little work being done on *Geranium*) the genus *Pelargonium* as well as its natural species includes many thousands of cultivars.

The nectar bearing tube remains, although difficult to see, being a slight bump where the flower stalk almost halves in size, but the simple irregular flower shape of the species, has been replaced by the rounded, single, semi-double, double, quilled and many other fancy shapes of the modern cultivars. The seed dispersal technique remains the most easily distinguishable method of identification for the average gardener.

The species within *Pelargonium* are remarkable for their ability to retain moisture and survive long periods of drought, an obvious adaptation of the plant to the conditions in which it grows in its natural habitat.

Among the species within *Pelargonium* there were sufficient plants with further common characteristics of habit, leaf and flower, for them to be further classified. Botanists such as Harvey (1860) and Knuth (1912) used the following classification of Section (Sub-genus) within *Pelargonium*. There are fifteen such Sections and these are:— *Hoarea: Seymouria: Polyactium: Otidia: Ligularia: Jenkinsonia: Myrrhidium: Peristera: Campylia: Dibrachya: Eumorpha: Glaucophyllum: Ciconium: Cortusina:* and *Pelargium*. Such botanical classification is primarily of interest to the student of botany, however three Sections *Ciconium, Dibrachya* and *Pelargium* are of interest to the average gardener because of their influence on the pelargoniums grown today.

Section *Ciconium* comprises plants described as half-shrubs or shrubs with thick and fleshy stems, among which are the ancestors of the well known zonal pelargonium.

Section *Dibrachya* comprises plants described as having weak, thin and slender stems mostly supported by other plants. Leaves fleshy and peltate (shield shaped) or cordate (heart shaped). Among these are the ancestors of the ivy-leaved pelargonium.

Section *Pelargium* comprises plants described as shrubs or half-shrubs with woody, branched or very much branched stems, among which are the ancestors of the regal pelargonium.

The fascination of these early South African discoveries and the subsequent recognition by 17th and 18th century nurserymen and gardeners, of the endless possibilities of cross pollination and breeding programmes, caused what became known in the 19th century as the pelargonium craze. Many hundreds of cultivars were introduced, some good, some mediocre, several standing the test of time and continuing to be listed in catalogues around the world today.

In the resurgence of interest after World War II the *Pelargonium* has again become the popular plant of the people. Further breeding programmes are being carried out and once again many beautiful hybrids are available to the gardening public.

New and beautiful cultivars attract the attention of the gardener; the unusual characteristics of the species, the discerning collector. At the present time there is an increasing awareness by gardeners and collectors of the name of a plant, be it cultivar or species, and the need for such name to be correctly stated.

When it is realized that in the world today there are about 300 000 plant species, together with an innumerable number of named cultivars, it becomes apparent that some form of guidance in plant taxonomy is necessary, not only for the botanist, hybridizer, introducer and nurseryman, but for the home gardener as well.

An organization known as The International Bureau for Plant Taxonomy has published two Codes: the International Code of Botanical Nomenclature, which governs the use of botanical names in Latin form and the International Code of Nomenclature of Cultivated Plants which aims to promote uniformity, accuracy and fixity in the naming of horticultural cultivars which are normally given fancy names.

Whilst botanical names in Latin form are written in italics, horticultural names, being fancy names, are written with capital initial letters for all words of the name (except where linguistic usage demands otherwise), and enclosed within single quotation marks.

Several registration authorities exist for cultivated plants, including the appointment in recent years, of an International Registration Authority for *Pelargonium*. The work of this Authority entails publishing a list of all known *Pelargonium* cultivar names, and the acceptance and approval (or otherwise) of proposed new names submitted for registration. Enquiries regarding this Authority may be directed to the Australian Geranium Society (see Appendix 2). Research for this Check List and Register of *Pelargonium* cultivar names has already established over 15 000 such names. Some of the plants bearing these names are not in circulation today but many are, and the problem of duplication of name within genus *Pelargonium* arises.

Modern marketing of plants, with the introduction of self-service garden centres, has created the need for customers to have some knowledge of the plants for which they are looking. This, together with the ability to identify those plants and to know their "fancy" names, makes the self-service procedure much easier. Naturally it is to be assumed, or at least hoped, that the plant purchased is correctly named, however among *Pelargonium* there may be some duplication of cultivar names.

Duplication of names was, almost certainly, brought about in earlier times by the lack of communication between countries, and by the then use, and continuing use, of the terms "geranium" and "pelargonium" for plants which botanically are all members of the genus *Pelargonium*.

The genus is a large and popular one, with thousands of cultivars being developed from the species within the three main Sections, *Ciconium*, *Dibrachya* and *Pelargium*. Whilst there has been some cross pollination between the Sections, the majority of cultivars have remained sufficiently distinctive of their group. For easy identification and classification genus *Pelargonium* has been horticulturally divided into four main groups, these being ZONAL; IVY-LEAVED; REGAL and SPECIES DERIVED (Spp.d.) PELARGONIUMS.

ZONAL PELARGONIUMS

Zonal pelargoniums are those plants commonly called "geraniums", "garden or bedding geraniums", Stork's bill" or "Fish or Horseshoe Geraniums". Their popularity stems from the wide range of flower colour and form, leaf shape and ornamentation, and growth habit. Their many uses in the garden, for pot plant culture, and for decorative work in the home, are outlined in further chapters in this book.

Flowering Zonal Pelargoniums

Flowering zonal pelargoniums include all those plants having any of the following characteristics of flower shape or form, and which are grown principally for their flowers:

SINGLE: having not more than five petals.
SEMI-DOUBLE: having more than five petals, but not more than eight.
DOUBLE: having more than eight petals.
ROSEBUD: having flowers which resemble the bud of a rose, being fully double and hearted, the middle petals remaining unopened.
QUILLED: having flowers, the petals of which are twisted into a quill. Sometimes known as "Cactus" or "Poinsettia".
BIRD'S EGG: having flowers, the petals of which are spotted like a bird's egg.
FIVE-FINGERED: having distinctive flowers and leaves, creating an impression of being either five-fingered or star-shaped. Variously known as "Both's Staphs", "The Staphs" or "Stellars". Included in this group are those plants having similarly distinctive flowers and foliage and variously known as "Fingered Flowers", "Formosa", "Miller's Formosum Hybrids" or "Bodey's Formosum Hybrids".

The reader may also find in books and catalogues other group names applied to smaller units of plants having some similarities. These include:

FIAT: having flowers, the petals of which have serrated edges.
IRENE: having semi-double to double chalice or cup-shaped flowers, and heavy-wooded growth.
PAINTED LADY: having flowers with a prominent white centre or eye. (Similar plants were known as Cyclops in the 1800's.)
NOSEGAY: having small narrow petalled flowers forming a large flower head (truss or inflorescence) and giving the appearance of a "bouquet". This is rather misleading for "nosegay" is usually associated with a bunch of sweet scented flowers. The term is now seldom used.

Among purists and collectors some plants are referred to by the name of the originator: for example, "Miller's hybrids", "Both's hybrids", "Bodey's hybrids" and in similar vein "The Deacons".

The term English or Standard, and French or Bruant are also sometimes used. These refer to growth habit and flower form; the English or Standard being of thin stemmed growth with the single flowers being more rounded, and the double more double than the French or Bruant type. These latter are heavy-wooded plants with flowers inclined to be chalice or cup-shaped; for example the IRENES. It has been recorded that the French type occurred spontaneously in France in the late 1800's, coming from the English type. These strong growing plants are also sometimes referred to as "gros bois" (heavy-wooded) and have become connected with the name of a famous hybridiser of the time, named Bruant, although it is not known that he originated the type.

Fancy-leaved zonal, flowering dwarf, miniature and micro-miniature zonal pelargoniums are rarely, if at all, found in the French or Bruant group.

Fancy-Leaved Zonal Pelargoniums

Fancy-leaved zonal pelargoniums are those plants grown primarily for the beauty of their leaves which show marked variations of colour, together with, or other than, green, as their normal growth habit.

For ease of identification the various colour combinations are here listed and described:

SILVER: having green leaves, sometimes covered with a silvery sheen, and edged more or less widely with white or cream.
SILVER TRICOLOUR: having leaves with similar markings of white/cream as the silver leaved group, but with added shadings of pink, red to purple. In addition there is often a dark red/chestnut zone. These are the most delicately coloured of all fancy-leaved zonal pelargoniums. Generally they are slow growing, need some protection from strong summer

sun, but give of their best during autumn, winter and early spring.

GOLD: having leaves without any trace of zoning or other markings and either yellow/gold or green/yellow.

GOLDEN TRICOLOUR: having leaves vividly marked with many colours, and with the zone usually clearly marked in red or bronze, and with added shades of red, yellow and crimson-lake. The outer edges, in most cases, being golden yellow rather than white or cream as in the silver tricolours. Considered by many collectors as the most brilliantly ornamental of the fancy-leaved group.

BRONZE: having leaves either gold or golden/green with prominent bronze to chestnut zoning or centre blotching.

BLACK: having leaves giving the appearance of being black or deep purple/black, or alternatively having a distinct black zone, or centre black blotch, on green.

BUTTERFLY-ZONE: having leaves with an irregular shaped mark in the centre of the leaf in the shape of a butterfly, and in a contrasting colour to the remainder of the leaf.

The normal height range of the zonal pelargonium is considered to be more than 20.3 cm (8″) at maturity. Many, depending on the particular cultivar, will grow even higher, others remain about the 20.3 cm height or even a little under. Usually classed as being dwarf growing. Several flowering and fancy-leaved zonals come into this category.

The two further height classifications of the zonal pelargonium are Miniature and Micro-Miniature.

MINIATURE: being those plants naturally miniature in leaf form, with short-noded stems and slow, compact growth which at maturity does not exceed 12.7 cm (5″) in height.

MICRO-MINIATURE: being those plants naturally more miniature in leaf form, shorter-noded stems and slower, more compact growth which at maturity does not exceed 7.6 cm (3″) in height.

A mature plant is one that has been cultivated under reasonably normal conditions for twelve months.

Two important points to note are that the fancy-leaved zonals, either normal, miniature or micro-miniature, are more limited in their range of flower shape, colour and form, than the flowering zonals. The flower of the fancy-leaved group being mainly in single or double forms with a few newer introductions in semi-double form. Also the flowers of the miniature and micro-miniature group, whilst originally developed in miniature size, in keeping with the leaf and overall characteristic of the plant, are now being produced with flowers of normal size, yet with the plant still remaining within the height limits of these two groups.

IVY-LEAVED PELARGONIUMS

The ivy-leaved pelargoniums are those plants commonly known as "ivy geraniums" but more correctly classified as ivy-leaved pelargoniums. They have succulent shield shaped leaves and trailing, sprawling and sometimes climbing (with support) habit. Modern cultivars come in a wide range of flower colour including white, pink, red, mauve and purple. In flower form they may be either:

SINGLE: having flowers with not more than five petals, usually more loosely arranged than the zonal pelargonium.

SEMI-DOUBLE: having more than five petals, but not more than eight, loosely arranged.

DOUBLE: having more than eight petals, some being loosely arranged and others tightly forming a rosette or rosebud shape.

Ivy-leaved pelargoniums also come in fancy-leaved forms, but in a more limited range than the flowering zonals:

SILVER: having leaves green in colour, either bordered or marked with white or cream.

GOLD: having leaves yellow/gold or green/yellow variously marked or edged with gold or bronze.

MESHED: having leaves green in colour, the veins of which are distinctly marked in white or cream.

The habit of growth of the ivy-leaved pelargoniums is given in the three categories here listed:

COMPACT: stems having short distances between the nodes.

LONG-TRAILING: having strong stems with long distances between the nodes.

MINIATURE: having thin stems extremely short jointed, compact growth, and miniature leaf and flower form.

Two further classifications affecting the zonal and ivy-leaved pelargoniums include:

HYBRID-ZONAL: those plants resulting from a zonal X ivy parentage, and showing clear characteristics favouring the zonal parent.

HYBRID-IVY: those plants resulting from a zonal X ivy parentage, and showing distinctive characteristics favouring the ivy-leaved parent. These are a small group but a rewarding one, being of compact growth, free flowering and Rust resistant.

REGAL PELARGONIUMS

Regal pelargoniums are those plants commonly known as "Pelargoniums", "Regals" and "Martha Washingtons" in the USA. Strong growing, bushy almost shrub-like, when in flower they are often likened to azaleas. The optimum flowering season is spring and early summer with a further short flowering late summer. Flowers are large, usually with a distinctive blotching or feathering. The dominant colour of the early regals was in the mauve/purple shades, being influenced mainly by the relationship to *Pelargonium cucullatum* one of its ancestors. Modern hybridizers have, and are, producing plants of the most exquisite colours and combinations of colours, together with others which have petals of soft pure colour without blotching or feathering, and some in fully double form. Growth habit has also been improved and many new cultivars have more compact growth than the older favourites which tend to become leggy if not pruned and shaped regularly. Flowering has been extended and it would appear that the future of the regal pelargonium has been assured.

Two further classifications within regal pelargoniums are:

FANCY-LEAVED: those plants having leaves showing marked variations of colour together with, or other than, green, as their normal growth habit.

MINIATURE: those plants having flowers and leaves similar to the normal regal but being miniature in form and with compact growth. Sometimes known as "Pansy Pelargoniums".

SPECIES DERIVED (Spp.d.)

The species derived pelargoniums are those plants showing a close relationship to the species from which they have been derived and which do not fit clearly into any of the above classifications. Included are the ANGEL, UNIQUE, SCENTED-LEAVED cultivars and the "ZONQUIL" pelargoniums.

ANGEL: those plants which, whilst having some similarity to the miniature regal pelargonium, are more closely associated with the species *Pelargonium crispum* which they resemble in leaf shape and growth habit, and from which many have been derived. Their height rarely exceeds 25.4 cm (10″) their stems are thin and rather woody, their growth is bushy, and they have an optimum flowering season of spring and early summer, seldom flowering during the colder months of the year. Flowers are single, usually in the rose, purple and mauve shadings and often with the upper petals being one colour and the lower another. In the 1930's to 1940's many were developed by Mr Langley-Smith and these have become known as the "Langley-Smith hybrids".

UNIQUE: those plants, the parentage of which is somewhat obscure and confused. Generally speaking they show similarity to the upright growing scented-leaved pelargoniums, being shrubby and woody, sometimes straggly, and with leaves usually irregularly and deeply cut. Their flowers which are smaller than the regal, are usually blotched and/or feathered. Leaves often slightly perfumed, although not always pleasantly.

"ZONQUIL": those plants resulting from the crossing of zonal pelargonium cultivars with *Pelargonium quinquelobatum*. A small group of Australian origin, the early work being done by the late Mr E. Both and carried on by Mr L. Bodey. There are few, if any, available commercially.

SPECIES: The final group within *Pelargonium* and possibly to some readers, the most interesting. Whilst there are approximately 200 species, there are only a relatively small number of these which have been used in hybridization programmes, being mainly those which have influenced the modern zonal, ivy-leaved and regal pelargonium. The scented-leaved pelargoniums, the majority of which are species from which no cultivated hybrids have been derived, are sufficiently popular to warrant further mention here.

SCENTED-LEAVED PELARGONIUMS

The scented-leaved pelargoniums are those plants which are grown primarily for the perfume of their leaves. The leaf shape and growth habit varies to such a degree that it would be impossible to make any arbitrary groupings. There are some that are tall growing, some short, some with very small leaves, others with large hairy foliage. Some have leaves without distinct lobes or divisions, others have the finest fern-like foliage. The one principal feature they all have in common is a perfumed leaf which may, or may not, be considered pleasant. Some of the suggested perfumes include lemon, peppermint, apple, nutmeg or spice, rose, lime and pungent. Flowers are usually small, either white, pink, or varying shades of mauve, lavender or violet. The scented-leaved group seed readily and there are a large number of slightly varying forms, particularly of the upright *Pelargonium radens* (Syn. *P. radula*) type. There has been little purposeful hybridisation done to improve these species, but much has been done in the production of essential oil, particularly in France. Many are available commercially, seldom by their correct species name, but rather as lemon scented, apple scented, peppermint scented and etcetera.

The remainder of the species pelargoniums are

remarkable for their diversity of flower shape and colour, leaf shape and texture, and habit of growth. Only a few are generally available through commercial sources, but for the collector, worth seeking out. The adaptability of the species to hot, dry conditions or long seasons of drought combined with their unusual flower form and colour and their interesting growth habits, must surely be an invitation to the discerning hybridizer. Perhaps some will influence the garden pelargoniums of the twenty first century and beyond. An exciting and challenging thought!

3. PURCHASING PLANTS

The purpose of this chapter is to offer guidance to the reader in the assessment of plants prior to purchase. A few hints can always help get value for money and avoid the disappointment of buying a plant which is not as good as it should be.

Having read the earlier chapters you will be aware that the common name of "geranium" is misleading and that this book is mainly about the three main types of pelargoniums, namely **Zonal, Ivy-leaved** and **Regal**. Unfortunately too few nurserymen and other gardeners are so well informed even though the name *Pelargonium* has been in use for South African derived plants since the 1700's.

In assessing a plant for purchase the prime requirement is that it is free from disease and other disabilities which may cause its death or poor performance. This is applicable whether the plant is to be grown in a container or in the garden. However, some disabilities may be corrected and need not prevent the purchase of a plant provided you are willing to follow the cultural procedures given later in this book. Many growers who insist on correctly named plants are so pleased to see some of the rarer cultivars available that they will buy the plant in any condition, just to obtain the genetic material. Subsequent propagation and good cultural techniques can provide a healthy well grown plant in a season.

Listed below are some of the inspection procedures which may be carried out readily.

1. In practically any plant the root system causes the greatest problem as it is usually hidden in soil or equivalent. A plant without a well developed root system for its size and so firmly anchored in the pot is not a good buy. A poor root system may indicate one or more of several unacceptable conditions. Two of these are (a) that the plant is a stem cutting inserted into the soil and has not yet had time to develop a satisfactory root system, and (b) the roots have rotted away or disintegrated due to a disease.

As at least one disease commences with the root system and then travels up the stem of the plant, it is very necessary to be aware of this hidden problem. Experience has shown that well rooted plants in

7.5 cm pots and 10.0 cm pots (clay or plastic) will easily withstand being lifted by the stem without the pot separating from the soil. Large plants in 12.5 cm pots will also perform similarly. However, there is a tendency to pot on a plant from a small pot into a larger pot and offer it for sale immediately instead of waiting for the plant and its root system to develop. Plants are normally priced according to the pot size which is an indication of the time taken to grow them. However, miniature pelargoniums are, by their very nature, small and the pot size is small even though they may have taken quite a long time to grow. A knowledge of the growth habit of the plant is useful when assessing a purchase.

Ivy-leaved pelargoniums are often placed in oversize hanging baskets to allow for growth. Some judgement is needed here, the appearance of the leaves should be glossy green, fully expanded without wrinkles as an indication of a healthy plant.

All stems should be set firmly in the soil but some potting mixes are rather 'soft' and allow a slight wobble of even well rooted plants.

2. Stems should be examined by pressing between thumb and forefinger. If the tissue is soft and/or discoloured some infection is indicated and the plant is unlikely to survive. Some plants, e.g. regals and ivy-leaved have naturally occurring light brown sections on the stem but this is not soft and can be readily identified as healthy tissue.

3. The young leaves at the growing tip of the stems should be green. If there is any sign of blackness or apparent 'burn' at the tips the plant should be rejected as some disease organisms enter at the growing tip and travel through the plant.

A few yellow or partly yellow leaves at the lower end of the stem is not a serious problem. All leaves die at some time or other and yellow leaves may be picked off and discarded. The yellowing usually commences at the margin and progresses inwards over the entire leaf. This may be due to poor culture and can be corrected to minimise further deterioration.

Regal pelargoniums in particular, are subject to yellow brown sections in the leaf between the veins.

This is due to a fungus and usually localized to only part of the leaf. As it does not spread rapidly throughout the plant the infected leaves may be removed and discarded and the remainder of the plant treated with a fungicide.

4. The zonal pelargonium is subject to a disease called 'rust' which is dealt with in some detail in the appropriate chapter on *Pests, Pathogens and Problems*. This is very common in some parts of the Sydney area although there are some cultivars of the zonals which are rust resistant. These are named in the chapter on *Selected Species and Cultivars* and are very useful for growing in the garden.

There is little point in rejecting a plant with 'rust' on the leaves if you already live in an area where the disease is prevalent. The infected leaves may be stripped off and left in the nursery garbage can as there is no point in further aggravating the problem.

Enthusiastic pelargonium growers are always keen to have correctly named plants yet the source of these is rather limited. In general most plants are not named and are simply sold as "geraniums" red or pink. Others carry a name tag and perhaps the names are correct, perhaps not. The gardening public, prompted by information given at pelargonium shows, is becoming increasingly aware of the need for correctly named plants and it is only by demanding, from the nursery or plant sales centre, that the plants be named, that this service will improve.

If a wholesale nursery is prepared to have the plant name on one side of the label and the nursery name on the other it is some guarantee that the propagator is name conscious and careful. The illustrations and descriptive text elsewhere in this book will be of assistance to the buyer in selecting plants for use in both containers and garden.

For guidance on where correctly named plants may be obtained consult your local Society specialising in pelargoniums. A list of Societies is given in Appendix 2.

Due to limited accommodation in many nurseries plants are packed closely together which usually ruins their shape by producing long leafless stems, often bent and twisted. If you are prepared to devote some time to shaping and culture as given elsewhere in this book this is not sufficient reason to reject the plants. As mentioned previously it is the genetic material which is valuable, the training of this material is then in the hands of the grower.

It is not possible to list every variation likely to be encountered on all plant types. As a gardener you will be able to use discretion and experience to assess the problem potential of the plant using the above guidelines.

It is good practice to set up a quarantine station in your garden to isolate newly purchased plants from those already growing there and from one another. If disease does develop it is confined and the infected plant may be treated or destroyed without affecting the others. A quarantine station should be in an isolated part of the garden and be free from wind and with plenty of light. If the plant has been grown in a glasshouse or sheltered situation this period also allows time for it to become adjusted to local environment.

Water the plants carefully to avoid splashing water around, fertilize and watch them grow. Leave in quarantine for at least three weeks in spring–summer and six weeks in winter. Inspect every few days for any sign of disease. Good growth in spring–summer is an indication of healthy plants. After removal from quarantine it is often advantageous to repot into your own mixture to produce uniformity in cultural methods.

4. PRUNING & SHAPING

Correct pruning is an essential part of good culture of most pelargoniums. The sight of a healthy plant, covered in lush foliage with a profusion of flowers is the ideal achievement of pelargonium growers. A well maintained plant devoid of unsightly dead flower heads and diseased or dead stems is just reward for the time spent in applying correct cultural procedures. See below for specific recommendations.

Pruning of pelargoniums keeps the plants looking fresh and healthy by encouraging new growth. Each new shoot will produce flowers, so therefore the more shoots, the more flowers. Pruning is also necessary to shape the plant and to remove any dead or diseased parts. (The latter should be done as soon as it is noticed at whatever time of year to prevent the spread of disease pathogens.)

Healthy plant material removed by pruning may then be used for propagating new plants by cuttings (see chapter on *Propagation by Cutting*). Pelargoniums are best replaced by new plants from time to time as they become woody with age; it is therefore wise to grow a few cuttings for this purpose and, of course, they make attractive and economical gifts.

The general rule of pruning 'after flowering' applies to pelargoniums: in autumn, after the main flowering season of spring and summer. Pruning at this time allows the plants an extended period to make new growth so that the plant's energy can be channelled into flower formation at the onset of the warmer spring weather. Of course, pelargoniums pruned at any time of year will still make new growth, but in the winter this growth will make little headway, and in the spring, the first flush so prized by pelargonium growers will be sacrificed. Pruning may be done in summer if desired and another light prune done in late winter/early spring. The regals have two main flushes of flower, the first in spring and the second in early summer. After the second flush, flowering is then finished for the year, unlike zonals and ivy-leaves which flower more or less continuously throughout spring and summer (and even through the whole year in many parts of Australia).

In frost-prone areas plants pruned at this time need the protection of a glasshouse or other cover (see chapter on *Growing in Containers*) to prevent burning of the new shoots. Growers in frost-prone areas usually prune in early spring after the frosts are finished; alternatively, the plants may be pruned in summer to encourage new growth before the frosts set in and then a further cutting back is carried out in early spring.

Two types of pruning are commonly practised on pelargoniums: the cutting of stems or branches and the removal of growing tips by hand ('pinching').

The fast-growing types of pelargoniums benefit from a fairly hard cut-back annually—these include many of the zonal, regal and ivy-leaved cultivars.

TOOLS FOR PRUNING

A single-edged razor blade or sharp knife is recommended for cutting soft growth, with secateurs being used for the harder wood. It may be necessary to trim the latter type of cuts with the razor blade or knife, particularly those on an awkward angle which are difficult to cut cleanly with the secateurs. Sharp tools are recommended as they make a clean cut without damaging plant tissues. It is also important to use disinfected tools to prevent transfer of the disease pathogens from one part of the plant to another or from one plant to another. A simple way of achieving this is to dip the cutting part of the tool in methylated spirits, at least as often as between pruning two different plants.

General guidelines for pruning are given in points 1–9 below. This is followed by extra guidelines pertaining specifically to zonals (including dwarfs, miniatures and fancy-leaves), regals, ivy-leaves, hybrid ivies and scenteds.

1. Prune to an outward pointing bud. This encourages outward branching which is desirable firstly to make a nicely shaped plant and secondly to avoid cluttering up the inside of the plant with too much foliage. Pelargoniums need good air circu-

lation to minimize the condition of oedema and fungal diseases (see chapter on *Pests, Pathogens & Problems*).

2. Cut just above a node. The node is the part of the stem where the leaves are or have been attached and also where new branches originate (refer Appendix 1). Even if no shoot is present at the time of pruning, a slight bump on the node indicates its presence, thus allowing the application of point 1 above. If the cut is made too far above the node the piece of stem above the node will die and will then need to be removed. Or it may rot and this may travel quickly down the stem necessitating a cut above the next node down: this may be undesirable particularly in achieving the intended shape of the plant.

3. Remove crossing stems. Crossing stems are undesirable because they result in tangled foliage and rub against each other, wounding the plant and providing an opening for the possible entry of disease pathogens. They are also aesthetically undesirable for a show plant.

4. Remove dead or diseased parts. This is essential to maintain a healthy plant as disease spreads and dead parts are of no further use to the plant. The cut should be made at least 5 cm below the dead tissue to ensure the removal of any disease pathogens which will almost certainly have moved into the green tissue. If after making the cut, brown-coloured tissue can still be seen, cut further down until the cut surface is all green. If removing a branch that is dead for its entire length, make a clean cut where it joins onto the healthy branch.

5. New shoots that emanate from near ground level, or below the point on a stem where the cut is made, should be tip pruned by 'pinching': removal of the growing tip. This is usually done quite simply by using the thumb and one other finger—a finger-nail proving a useful tool. These new shoots are young and vigorous and will grow at the expense of newer shoots which will develop as a result of the pruning. By removing the growing tip at an early stage, the plant's energy will be channelled into a more uniform development of all shoots, resulting in a better shaped plant.

6. As each new shoot reaches three to four nodes in length, these should all be tip pruned to encourage further branching. 'Pinching' may be continued until about June (southern hemisphere)—May for fancy-leaved plants—to allow approximately eight weeks for flower development. Once the flower buds start to appear, selected 'pinching' should be continued throughout

spring and summer to maintain a desirably shaped plant.

7. It is desirable to seal newly cut surfaces with an alcohol-based solution (eg. methylated spirits)—this kills the top layer of cells thus preventing disease organisms from entering the plant. A dab using a cotton bud is a convenient method for this purpose. Alternatively, cut surfaces may be dusted with a fungicide.

8. The newly pruned plant will benefit from an application of fertiliser at this stage to encourage rapid production of shoots before the winter when the plant's growth is slowed (see chapter 6 on soil mixes for types of fertilizers).

9. Once the pruned plant starts to shoot, these shoots may be 'pinched' back to encourage further branching. This should be done when the shoots contain four or five nodes. (Many cultivars differ in their growth habits and discretion is often required in deciding when to 'pinch'.) If too many shoots are formed, especially facing into the middle of the plant, it may be necessary to remove some of these to allow sufficient air circulation—make a clean cut where the shoot joins onto the stem.

Zonals

The general guidelines numbered 1–9 above apply to zonal pelargoniums. Zonals can tolerate quite hard pruning, i.e. back to four or five nodes from soil level. They may even be taken back to three nodes, particularly if the nodes are spaced far apart and/or there are one or more shoots already emerging from near ground level.

Dwarf Zonals

Less severe pruning is required for this group of pelargoniums owing to their comparatively slow growth habit. Stems may be cut back to about one-third their length. It should be pointed out that the nodes on dwarf zonals tend to be quite close together and outward pointing buds are not as obvious as they are on the larger growing zonal pelargoniums. The cultivars also vary slightly in their growth habit, some tending to be more leggy than others. Discretion is therefore necessary in deciding how and where to prune. Again owing to their slow growth habit, tip pruning is not required to be carried out as frequently as on the more vigorous zonals, regals and ivy-leaves. Tip pruning is usually done on a branch that is observed to be growing faster than other branches on the plant, thus giving the plant a lopsided shape. Tip pruning in this instance aids in maintaining uniform growth.

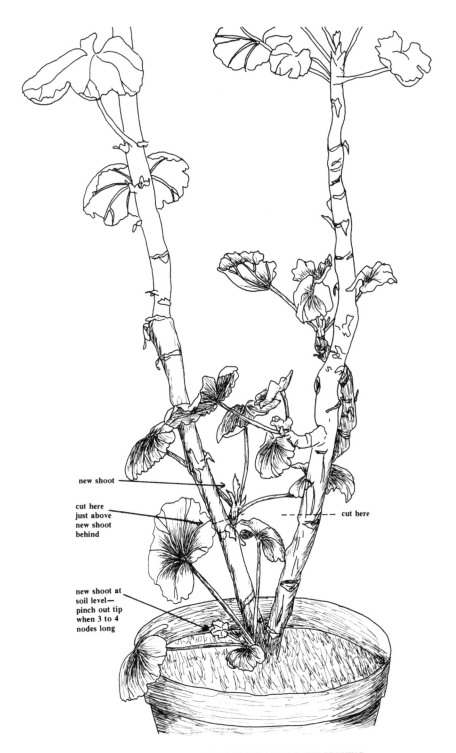

new shoot

cut here
just above
new shoot
behind

cut here

new shoot at
soil level—
pinch out tip
when 3 to 4
nodes long

ZONAL PELARGONIUM REQUIRING PRUNING

Miniatures

Miniature pelargoniums are more slow growing again than the dwarf types and do not usually need pruning in the normally accepted manner for pelargoniums (as described in the general guidelines above). They tend to branch of their own accord and form a bushy compact shape. Tip pruning may be done if required to maintain this compactness.

Fancy-Leaves

These plants are valued for the colourings in their foliage which are at their peak during the winter months. Therefore, in order to allow for sufficient time after pruning for foliage growth to develop, pruning is carried out in spring. The guidelines numbered 1–9 above also apply to fancy-leaved zonals. Tip pruning maintains the colour on new shoots formed.

Regals

In the case of regal pelargoniums, it is recommended that pruning be done in stages, remove approximately one-third the number of stems (cut into the reddish-brown coloured wood occurring between the green tip growth and the older brown wood at base of stem); wait a few weeks until these stems start to shoot; then remove another third of the plant and when these stems in turn start to shoot, complete the pruning of the final third.

This procedure is recommended particularly for regals three or more years of age. By this time the lower parts of the stems are developing into hard wood; there are no leaves left attached to this hard wood; if the entire top portion of the plant is removed all at the same time, this may be too much of a shock for the plant and it may not develop new shoots. By pruning the plant one-third at a time, this method allows it to continue manufacturing food for itself via the leaves left on the plant while the pruned part is putting out new shoots.

Although a plant pruned all over at once may grow satisfactorily, the procedure described above is less stressful on the plant. A plant under stress is more prone to attack by pests and diseases than a plant not under stress; therefore the benefits from pruning in such a manner become obvious.

Ivy-Leaves

It rather depends on the situation of ivy-leaved pelargoniums, and/or individual preferences, as to how hard they are pruned or even whether they are pruned at all. If grown in a location where long trailing stems are desired (sprawling over an embankment or hanging from a window box, for example) pruning may be bypassed and the plants simply given an occasional tidy-up by removing dead leaves and flowers, and cutting off dead branches.

For a more compact shape, it is recommended that tip pruning be commenced at the early stage of growth of a rooted cutting, when the plant has three to five nodes. This encourages branches to develop so that as the plant grows, it will have a number of stems emanating from near ground level, resulting in relatively uniform growth. To maintain a compact shape, the ivy-leaved cultivars may be pruned back to about one-third their size. The method of pruning one-third of the plant at a time, described for regals, above, may also be applied to ivy-leaved pelargoniums.

It should be pointed out that point 3 (remove crossing stems) of the general guidelines does not apply to ivy pelargoniums. This would result in far too much of the plant being removed and would be going against the plant's natural growth habit.

Hybrid Ivies

These plants tend to have a semi-sprawling habit and benefit from an annual prune back to about one-third their size, interspersed with tip pruning to keep bushy.

Scenteds

Many scented pelargoniums do not require pruning, either because they have a naturally branching growth habit (e.g. *Pelargonium tomentosum* and "Both's Snowflake"), or their growth habit is a compact clump (e.g. *P. odoratissimum*—apple; *P. grossularioides*—coconut). Most of the scenteds are in fact *Pelargonium* species which have evolved their own extremely varied growth patterns and tend to 'go their own way' regardless of any attempts to control their growth by pruning. However, many of the tall-growing types, or hybrid crosses, such as 'Lady Plymouth' and 'Mabel Grey' respond in the normal manner to pruning as outlined in the guidelines 1–9 above.

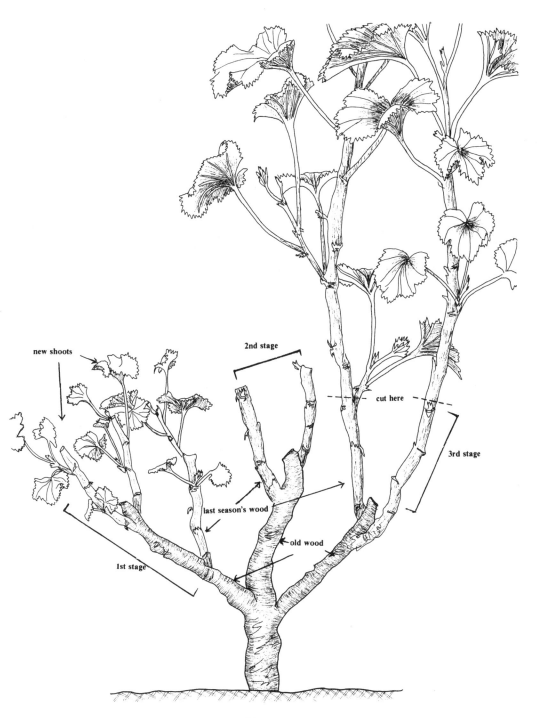

new shoots

2nd stage

cut here

3rd stage

last season's wood

old wood

1st stage

HOW TO PRUNE A REGAL PELARGONIUM

5. PROPAGATION BY CUTTING

There are many methods in commercial use at the present time for propagating plants. However, propagation of pelargoniums by a stem cutting remains, for the home gardener, the simplest way of obtaining a new plant exactly like its parent. For descriptions of other methods such as meristem culture, grafting, layering, etc., other texts specializing in these topics should be consulted.

It should also be briefly mentioned here that most new cultivars of pelargoniums are obtained by seed—either specifically hybridized for this purpose (see chapter on *Hybridization and growing from Seed*) or from chance seedlings that may appear in the garden as a result of cross-fertilization by insects.

Time cuttings are taken

Pelargonium cuttings may be rooted at any time of year in frost-free areas, but the optimum time is autumn, after the humidity of summer and before the cold of winter. This is convenient because it coincides with pruning time, thus providing the necessary plant material. In hot, humid weather, many cuttings fall prey to fungal diseases; in cold weather they take longer to form roots and may still die of fungal stem rot especially if kept damp for a protracted period.

Fancy-leaved cultivars, however, are usually pruned in spring. This is because these plants are grown primarily for the beauty of their foliage: the advent of cold temperatures (particularly at night) combined with sunny days, provide ideal conditions for the fancy-leaved cultivars to display the often vivid colourings in their leaves. Therefore, to obtain maximum colour during the winter months, the plants are best pruned the previous spring to allow them time to make sufficient growth for the following winter season.

Types of cuttings

Two main types of cuttings are commonly used in propagating pelargoniums: tip cuttings and stem cuttings. Tip cuttings comprise the top part of a stem; in the case of zonals, they are approximately 100 mm in length and may contain three or four nodes. Tip cuttings on regal and ivy-leaved pelargoniums may be longer than this owing to greater length of their internodes. For miniatures, a

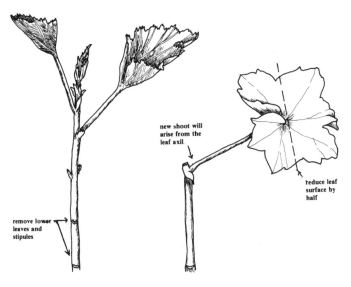

new shoot will arise from the leaf axil

reduce leaf surface by half

remove lower leaves and stipules

TIP CUTTING—REGAL PELARGONIUM   STEM CUTTING—IVY-LEAVED PELARGONIUM

typical length may be about 25 mm or even less, owing to the much shorter internodal space typical of their growth habit.

Stem cuttings comprise cut up sections of stem between a tip cutting and the cut where the branch has been pruned off the parent plant. Stem cuttings may contain as little as two nodes and it is desirable for the upper node to have a leaf attached. This not only shows at a glance the top and bottom ends of the cutting but the leaf also provides a root-inducing hormone. If desired, a sloping cut may be made at the top end of the cutting and a cut straight across made at the bottom end: this is common horticultural practice for establishing the polarity (which way is up!) of various types of stem cuttings.

It is essential that healthy plant material only be selected. Even a speck of diseased tissue will quickly spread and the cutting will soon rot and need to be discarded.

Tools

As pelargonium cuttings are particularly susceptible to fungal and/or bacterial stem rot, it is advisable to sterilize all tools used in taking cuttings. The ideal way of accomplishing this is to dip the cutting blade of the tool into methylated spirits and then pass it through a flame. If this method is used, caution is advocated: it will be obvious that naked flame is a potential fire hazard. The next best method is to simply dip the tools in methylated spirits alone. It is important to point out that other equipment that come in contact with the cuttings should also be sterilized.

Clean pots and crock should also be used—for the home gardener, washing thoroughly with water may be sufficient. If soaps or detergents are used, these should be rinsed off before using the pots.

Striking media

Pelargoniums have been known to form roots in a wide variety of media, from water to garden soil. However, coarse river sand remains a popular medium, being easily recognised and for the most part readily obtainable. After the cutting has rooted it may then be transferred to the garden bed or potted into a suitable mixture. Other substances such as vermiculite, clinker ash, blue metal screenings, peat pots and combinations of sand and peat moss have been successfully used to strike pelargoniums. Some growers like to strike their cuttings by placing them directly in the ground beside the parent plant—this has the advantages of immediate identification (assuming the parent plant is named) and quickness and ease of operation.

For pot culture, placing the cutting directly into a soil mix (preferably a well-aerated one) is also a proven satisfactory method. In similar fashion, a 10 cm pot may be filled with potting mix, a hole scooped in the middle and filled with coarse river sand—the cutting is then dibbled into the inner core of sand thus obviating the need for the first step in the process of potting on.

Pasteurization of media

As a further safeguard against disease, soil and/or cutting media may be pasteurized. Steam pasteurization is the best method—the home oven may be used for this purpose. Spread the media in a dampened state onto a tray (an old baking tray is ideal); place in oven pre-heated to 60°C (140°F) for half an hour exactly; remove and let cool before use; loosen with a clean fork to aerate the mix thus eliminating built-up toxic gases. A temperature of 60°C is sufficiently high to kill nematodes and most pathogenic bacteria and fungi. However, other organisms (beneficial) remain in the media and upon cooling they multiply rapidly, thus being in a favourable position to combat any disease pathogens that enter at a later date. If the soil is pasteurized, it then becomes necessary to use sterile tools and pots to avoid the introduction of disease organisms into the pathogen-free media. Such utensils may be washed in a 10% Formalin solution (1 part Formalin to 9 parts water).

If the more severe process of sterilization is used, this kills every living organism and if the media are reinfected with harmful pathogens (and the chances are very high that this will occur) they will reproduce in vast quantities with no beneficial organisms to stop their progress. (Some ovens have a lowest temperature setting of 65.6°C (150°F), in which case this temperature may be used provided the mix is removed promptly after the half hour.)

Method of striking tip cuttings

Firstly select portion of stem (approximately 100 mm, less or more, depending on type, as discussed earlier), cutting just below a node. An alternative method would be to cut *through* the node, but this requires a great deal of precision; there is more margin for error in making the cut just below the node. The cut is made here because there is a build-up of cambial tissue at the nodal joints from whence new roots and/or shoots arise.

Remove all but the top couple of new young leaves, including the stipules (refer Appendix 1). Also remove any flowers that may be present—this allows the cutting to channel its food reserves into root formation. (Cuttings may be kept in a dry condition for up to a day before inserting into medium.)

The cuttings may then be dusted with a fungicide

(e.g. Zineb) to minimise the risk of stem rot; it has been noted that when this procedure is followed, roots may take a little longer to form.

A dibbler or other suitable instrument should be used to make the hole for the cutting, only deep enough so that when the cutting is placed in the medium it is in intimate contact with it at the base as well as all around the sides. This is achieved by firming into place only deep enough to cover the bottom node.

Four or five tip cuttings will fit around the circumference of a 100 mm pot. Cuttings may also be grown in trays if lack of space is a problem. If desired, cutting pots or 'tubes' may be used with one cutting per pot—this has the advantage of minimum root disturbance when it comes time to pot on. It also prevents one diseased cutting from infecting all of the others, a disadvantage when using trays.

The media used for cuttings should be pre-wetted. This is best achieved by placing the pot or tray in a larger container of water, allowing the water to seep into the pot from the bottom and move up through the media (capillary action)—this has the advantage of not disturbing the cuttings by overhead watering. After watering in this fashion, only water again when the surface of the media feels quite dry. Cuttings take anything from four to fourteen days (sometimes a little longer) to form root, depending on individual cutting and time of year.

The cuttings should be placed in a warm, shady, protected place out of the wind until roots have formed.

There is some evidence to suggest that more rapid growth is obtained from pelargoniums if potted on immediately roots begin to appear. This is evidenced by concurrent growth of new leaves; when potted on at this time it has been observed that the bottom leaves on the plant remain green and are not shed. Other growers like to leave their cuttings until they have made substantial root with a consequent yellowing and loss of lower leaves when potting on. Either method has an equal chance of resulting in a healthy plant when mature: it lies with the individual to adopt whichever method suits him/her and the prevailing conditions best.

When potting on or planting in the garden, pelargonium tip cuttings usually need to be tip pruned to encourage immediate side branching (for further details, see *Pruning and Shaping*).

Method of striking stem cuttings

The procedure for striking tip cuttings may be followed with these exceptions:
Firstly, remove leaf (and/or shoot) from lower node and cut leaf on upper node in half. This reduces transpiration (water loss) thus helping to keep the cutting alive until it develops roots (one of their functions being the absorption of water). The removal of the leaf and/or shoot from the lower node also indicates immediately the polarity of the cutting, as it is most important that the cutting be inserted in the medium the right way up.

Secondly, stem cuttings, being harder wood than tip cuttings, usually take a little longer to root: it is therefore recommended that stem cuttings be grown in a separate container from tip cuttings so that when each type of cutting is tipped out for re-potting, all of that type will have formed roots at roughly the same time.

New growth appears from the bud in the leaf axil when these types of cuttings begin to form root. Even if there is no axillary bud evident when the cutting is inserted, it will soon appear (assuming the cutting forms root).

All cuttings

Hormone rooting powders or solutions may be used if desired, although there is some debate about whether or not these products do indeed speed up the rooting process. If they are used, in order to give the cutting fungicide protection, it then becomes necessary to drench the medium with a fungicide suspension, as opposed to dusting the cutting with a fungicide powder. This may be done prior to the insertion of cuttings. Some growers consider this method of fungicide application more advantageous in any case, because it permeates the entire containerful of sand (or other media) as well as being totally absorbed by the cutting, as opposed to a dry application at the basal end of the cutting.

The use of bottom heat may prove beneficial in areas that have a long winter period, to extend the time propagating may take place. As a general rule the root area should be warmer than the top of the cutting with optimum temperatures of $23°-27°C$ ($75°-80°F$) and $21°C$ ($70°F$) respectively. Small electrically heated propagating boxes are commercially available. However, pelargoniums root very easily and if the above procedures are followed, such propagating aids are not necessary.

Labelling

It is a good idea to label the cuttings as soon as they are taken with their cultivar name and the date. Packets of plastic labels are available at selected nurseries, garden centres and other stores, and indelible felt-tip pens are also on the market.

Note

Other vegetative methods of propagating pelargoniums include nodal, leaf bud and heel cuttings, not outlined in this text.

6. POTTING MIXES & NUTRIENTS

It is common practice to refer to the material in which container plants grow as the 'potting mix' or 'potting compost' rather than soil as some of the mixtures contain little or no soil at all.

Many readers, some of whom may have grown plants, in pots, using garden soil, may wonder why special potting mixtures are needed. A plant in a pot is basically growing under un-natural conditions, its root run is restricted, drainage could well be deficient and the limited nutrients may be readily exhausted. To overcome these restrictions growers have, over the years, evolved various mixtures, with added nutrients, in which to cultivate plants. Many variations and combinations are possible, and the grower may select one or more of these to suit his or her needs for satisfactory plant culture.

Whichever combination of ingredients is used the ultimate aim is to ensure optimum growing conditions for the plant grown by you in your own place. Many gardeners use large quantities of compost to build up the quality of soil, others use very little or none, some have near plain sand, others have near pure clay all of which goes to make the specification of garden soil very variable. That which is high in compost can most certainly be used, with a careful watch on the acidity of this and with the addition of nutrients as required.

The aim of this chapter is to list and review many of the substances which may be used to make a potting mix. The attributes of these are given together with possible deficiencies to watch out for, so enabling the reader to exercise discretion in creating a mix suitable for local conditions.

Three typical potting mixtures are given, any of which growers may like to try out before embarking on the creation of their own recipes. These will also serve as a rough guide to relative quantities of the raw materials to use when creating your own recipes. It is essential that all raw materials and fertilizers added must be thoroughly mixed to avoid pockets of any material. The simplest way of doing this is to use a large mixing board, such as a piece of masonite, turning and turning over the raw materials first to ensure an even distribution of each one. The fertilizers are then added, one at a time,

turning over the mix to distribute these evenly throughout. A plastic garbage-can provides a useful storage container for the completed mix. In order to facilitate both biological and chemical action in the mix it should be stored in a slightly damp condition.

Typical mixes

1. A mix without soil, it drains well and usually requires watering every three or four days. It must be kept damp (not soggy) otherwise it is difficult to wet and applied water runs through the pot without wetting the mix.

1 part of coarse sand	1 part is equivalent
2 parts of peat moss	to a full 4.5 litre
1 part dry cow manure	(1 gallon) container.

4 parts blood and bone	
2 parts superphosphate	1 part = 50 millilitre
1 part of potash	measuring glass
3 parts of dolomite	
Water to dampen mix.	

2. A mix which uses soil plus organic matter. It should hold water for a week particularly in plastic pots.

4 parts of sandy loam	
1 part of leaf mould	
1 part of cow manure	part measures
1 part of rice hulls	as above
½ part of charcoal pieces about 1–2 cms size	

4 parts blood and bone	
2 parts superphosphate	part measures
1 part potash	as above
1 part dolomite	
Water to dampen mix	

3. A mix without soil. It must be kept moist otherwise it is difficult to wet. It should hold water for a week unless conditions are very hot and dry.

2 parts of peat moss
2 parts of coarse sand
½ part vermiculite   part measures
½ part of charcoal pieces   as above
   about 1–2 cms size
½ part of cow manure

4 parts of blood and bone
2 parts of superphosphate   part measures
3 parts of dolomite   as above
1½ parts of potash
Water to dampen mix

For those without facilities for preparing a mix one of the ready made mixtures sold in plastic sacks may be purchased. Although all of these have not been tried out, the ones used were not impressive. Perhaps these could have been improved by additives. One major problem seemed to be their 'oiliness' and they were difficult to wet properly with ordinary surface watering. Perhaps the dipping of the pot into a bucket of water may have been successful.

The raw materials

The following substances may be used as the major components of a potting mix in varying proportions. By studying the characteristics of these materials the actual quantities to be used may be estimated to suit the plants and cultural methods desired, that is, frequency of watering, type of container, sunny, shady, windy locations and so on.

1. **Loams**   There is no soil particle called a 'loam'. It is a mixture of three basic soil particles—sand, silt and clay.

Types of Loam	composition (per cent)		
	sand	silt	clay
Sandy loam	75	10	15
Loam	40	35	25
Clay loam	35	30	35

Also 'Loam' does not mean a black soil or a soil rich in organic matter as many people believe.

The above three types of loam may also be described, after wetting, as follows:

Sandy loam—particles cohere yet is easily friable, individual grains can be felt

Loam—coherent and friable-sand grains cannot be felt in moist sample

Clay loam—much more plastic than loam, not easily friable.

The greater the sand content the easier the drainage, the greater the clay content the greater the water retaining ability but the less the airspace available to the root system. For *Pelargonium* culture it is usual to add coarse sand to a clay loam

although experience has shown that this is not always mandatory as other additives may break up the clay loam sufficiently.

2. **Compost**   Compost from the heap or bin may be used freely in the potting mix. It has a high cationic exchange capacity, that is, it can retain a large amount of nutrients and give these up to the roots when needed. During the continued breakdown of compost, acids are formed which may, after a period of time, make the potting mix too acid. This destroys the capacity of the organic matter to release nutrients it holds so the acidity must be counteracted by the addition of dolomite. This is one reason why dolomite has been included in the three typical mixes given previously. If anything more than mild acidity is encountered the *Pelargonium* will cease growth and perhaps the leaves will yellow and the plant look poorly. This condition may be corrected by re-potting or by adding a small quantity (about fifteen grams or ½ ounce) of dolomite to the top of the pot and watering in. The desirable condition is just slightly acid with a pH value of between 6.5 and 7. A value lower than 6.5 is too acid for proper growth.

Providing that this mildly acid condition is maintained the compost will continue to break down and form humus in the container. Humus acts as a chelating agent preventing some nutrients from being bound up in the mix and so unavailable to the plant.

3. **Peat Moss**   Finely shredded or 'rubbed up' peat moss is used quite a lot in mixes of all sorts. It provides some water retention if it is not allowed to dry out, whereupon it becomes difficult to wet with limited quantity of water flow. The water flows around the peat moss without wetting it through.

Any mix using peat moss should be well supplied with dolomite as the peat moss, in time, produces considerable acidity in the mix. Yellow leaves or lack of growth after the plant has been four to six months in a peat moss mix indicates a possible high acidity. A dose of dolomite, as stated under the heading for Compost, is needed to correct this condition.

4. **Charcoal**   Small charcoal pieces of about 1 to 2 cms are recommended and larger pieces should be broken up to about this size. Charcoal is an inert substance but has very good water retention ability due to its porous nature. Measurements have shown that charcoal holds as much water as clay but the plant root can extract 35% more water from charcoal than it can from clay. This is largely due to the enormous comparable surface area of clay particles and their small size. In addition to

containing water charcoal retains nutrients in solution so providing a reserve of these in the mix. However, heavy watering will wash these out of the pot as charcoal has very little cationic exchange capacity. Prior to use the charcoal should be washed in a bucket of water to remove fine particles and any other impurities. Where plant culture requires a long interval between watering, charcoal should be added to the potting mix to form a water reservoir.

5. **Rice Hulls** This is another product obtainable in a large sack for a few dollars from orchid nurseries where it is used extensively in potting mixtures. It promotes drainage and increases air space in the mix, however mixes using it should either have the nitrogen supply increased or be watered frequently with a water soluble fertilizer containing nitrogen. The quantity of rice hulls used should not exceed about one eighth of the total mix volume.

6. **Vermiculite** This has been used extensively in potting mixes largely to improve the drainage and water holding capacity. It is a very light weight substance and holds several times (about six) its own weight of water. It is also an active ion exchanger, holding nutrients until they are required by the root system whereupon these nutrients are then released. In this respect it is not unique, as organic matter in composts also acts in this way. However, the release of nutrients held by vermiculite is not so dependent on the pH value (acidity) as is compost. In this respect vermiculite is a valuable additive, particularly for growers who cannot measure the pH of the mix, as it does ensure the release of nutrients in an acid mix. The potash content of the mix should be increased when using vermiculite as this tends to bind up potassium, so making it unavailable. This is overcome by saturating the binding sites with potassium leaving the remainder in the mix available to plants.

7. **Seaweed** This substance has not received much attention as an additive to potting mixes but for those having a supply available it is worth considering. It should, of course, be washed thoroughly with tap water over a drain to remove surface salt which is very deleterious to the potting mix and to plants. It should be chopped as small as convenient and added to the mix. It contains a lot of potassium and other substances for the promotion of bacterial growth. However, as this growth temporarily depletes the mix of nitrogen to the detriment of plant growth, extra nitrogenous fertilizer should be added to the potted plant. There is no need to add this until the plant is placed in the pot or if the mix is not used for plants for some two months after mixing.

Hidden bonuses are (a) the 20 to 30% alginic acid contained in the seaweed is an active promoter of crumb structure in the mix and (b) seaweed contains chelated trace elements. This means these are not bound up in a hard-to-get-at form in the mix but remain always available to the plant.

8. **Sand** Sand is divided into two types. Coarse sand of particle size between 2 mm and 0.2 mm and fine sand of particle size between 0.2 mm and 0.02 mm. Reference to sand in potting mixtures means coarse sand, usually spelt out as coarse river sand, implying its freedom from salt. It is used to promote good drainage in soils, however, if a sandy loam is used it already contains a lot of sand so further addition is unnecessary. If clay loam or loam is used some sand should be added.

9. **Cow manure** This is given in this section because it is used in quantities similar to the rest of the raw materials. It provides some nitrogen and potassium and releases organic acids which chelate or combine with nutrients, particularly iron, to prevent this being 'fixed' in the mix and rendered unavailable.

10. **Leaf Mould and Bark** Both are good additives but require extra nitrogen to feed the fungus breaking down the harder materials and extra dolomite to counter the acidity produced by these components. The drainage is improved by these substances and they are worth using but the characteristics of each depend very much on the source of material. Probably the answer is to use sparingly until satisfied with the result.

Nutrients

These are the substances (often called fertilizers) added to the mixture and are part of the recipe. The three nutrients needed in the greatest quantities are Nitrogen, Phosphorus and Potassium often referred to as N-P-K.

In the nursery trade and for private growers with hundreds of pots, fertilizing is a labour intensive business, hence costly, so these growers often prefer to include a slow release fertilizer such as Osmocote or Nutricote, into the potting mix. Slow release means release over four to five months or eight to nine months, depending on your selection. Slow release fertilizers contain all three substances N, P and K and should be used in accordance with the directions for perennials. Although slow release fertilizers have been incorporated into a mix, other fertilizing action may be required during the growing and flowering life of the plant. Other chapters deal with this matter.

The following is a brief commentary on the major nutrients.

1. **Nitrogen** If the mix contains considerable organic matter this will eventually decompose releasing nitrogen as ammonia which hopefully, in a moist mix, will combine with the phosphate instead of escaping into the atmosphere. However, if the mix is used before decomposition, say before two months, extra nitrogen will need to be added. Dried blood, blood and bone or water soluble fertilizers containing urea are very useful.

Decomposition of organic matter is done by bacteria and fungi both of which have the first call on available nitrogen so the plant suffers if there is not enough for all.

2. **Phosphorus** All the sample mixes given contain superphosphate. Phosphorus is a very important nutrient responsible for many aspects of plant growth including genetic material, cell multiplication and usage of sugars. Superphosphate is relatively insoluble in water so if added in excess it will not suddenly increase the salt content of the mix and damage the roots.

3. **Potassium** The release of Potassium from soils and other natural sources is usually too slow for good growth, particularly in the limited space of a pot. Additional potassium needs to be added usually in the form of chloride or sulphate. The sulphate is absorbed by the plant rather less readily and tends to acidify the mix slightly.

4. **Other nutrients** Of these iron is the most likely to show as a deficiency (see chapter on *Pests, Pathogens and Problems*). This may be corrected by applying a weak solution of iron chelates to the potted plant. Other minor elements are usually present in commercial fertilizers and in sufficient quantity to obviate deficiencies. Water soluble fertilizers often contain these elements.

Acidity and its control by dolomite or lime

In this chapter frequent reference has been made to acidity of the mix and the suitable pH range for pelargoniums. This is one of the most important aspects of container culture and some explanation is needed to permit growers to control this factor.

The acid value, or pH, can only be applied to water solutions so reference to soil pH, bark pH and so on means the pH value of the solution surrounding these solids, that is water, the pH of which is influenced by the acids (or Hydrogen ions) dissolved in it.

Values of pH vary from 0 to 14 but in gardening only a small part of this is used namely from pH 5 to pH 8 (the former being much more acid than the latter). Various pH test kits are on the market some of which test over a range of 2 to 11. This means that a lot of the range is useless to the gardener and the wide range decreases the accuracy of the readings taken. The acquisition of such a device is a worthwhile investment and allows the intelligent application of substances to correct excessive acidity.

As pH values are based on the common logarithm, a pH value of 6 is 10 times more acid than a pH value of 7, and a pH value of 5 is 100 times more acid than a pH value of 7. The greater the acidity the lower the pH value, the reason for this is outside the scope of this book.

An important part of acidity correction and one seldom mentioned is buffering. This is the ability of a solution to resist a rapid change in pH and soil solutions are buffered to varying extents. A solution in sand is poorly buffered and requires only 450 grams of lime (or 670 grams of dolomite) to raise a volume of 130 litres from pH 5.5 to 6.5. The same quantity of potting mix (or soil) rich in organic matter requires 1120 grams of lime (or 1700 grams of dolomite) to raise the pH over the same range. This latter is well buffered.

Dolomite is generally preferred to lime where the costing is not significant as dolomite contains magnesium, an essential plant element.

Water

This is such a common material that few realize it supplies one nutrient to the plant, that is Hydrogen. It is of course required for many other purposes and is usually in plentiful supply. However, there is one harmful substance sometimes dissolved in it, namely common salt. In some areas the natural water is 'hard' having a magnesium and calcium carbonate content. To assist the housewife the supply to the house is passed through a water softener to remove these substances. Co-incident with this removal sodium ions are added to the water and this is harmful to both the plant and mix. It is far preferable to use water from the tap on the 'hard' side of the water softener.

In some country districts, particularly in drought periods water from the river has a high salt content which is again detrimental and rain water, if available, should be used in lieu of river water. Rain water contains many substances useful as plant fertilizers, washed down from the industrial polluted atmosphere. Bore water can be rather alkaline and should be avoided if rain water can be substituted. If bore water is known to be alkaline, citric acid should be added. Without pH measurement the exact quantity cannot be specified but 200 milligrams to 4 litres of water will reduce the pH by about 1.6 in unbuffered water. 200 milligrams of citric acid is just enough to cover a one cent piece without heaping. The exact quantity is not very critical as citric acid is fairly docile and a little too much is not harmful.

Conclusion

Creating a recipe for a potting mix with the intelligent application of the attributes and deficiencies of the raw materials can be most rewarding and doubly so when the plants grow and bloom to near perfection.

7. GROWING IN CONTAINERS

Pot plant culture has a long history going back thousands of years and there would appear to be a resurgence of this form of gardening in recent times, pelargoniums being among the most common specimens grown in containers.

There are many advantages of growing in pots: the ability to move plants around: for example, plants that have just been pruned can be placed in an inconspicuous part of the garden until they look attractive again; as the seasons change a plant may be moved to take advantage of more (or less) sunlight; a pelargonium in bloom may be used to decorate a place in the garden to draw attention away from other plants which are out-of-season; window boxes may be kept permanently attractive by potted plants placed temporarily in the box while they are looking their best; potted pelargoniums may be brought inside as occasional decoration (while sunrooms and other light airy places in the house may provide a suitable environment for keeping potted pelargoniums for a considerable length of time, they should not be kept in an internal—and therefore darker—room for more than a day or two); and, of course, potted specimens are necessary for those enthusiasts who like to exhibit at shows and other functions.

The choice of container may only be limited by imagination and/or availability. The main requirements are that it should be able to hold the soil (or other growing media), should not be toxic to the plants and should provide adequate drainage.

CONTAINER MATERIALS

Terracotta Clay pots remain popular with many people largely because they typify 'the traditional pot'. For *Pelargonium* usage, they have two main advantages. Their weight prevents top-heavy plants from toppling over (the regals in particular quickly develop top-heavy foliage and if in light-weight pots, are blown over even in a light breeze). Their porosity aids in a comparatively rapid drying out of the soil, desirable for pelargoniums which are particularly prone to stem rot if kept in overly moist conditions for too long a period (see chapter on *Pests, Pathogens & Problems*). Another advantage of clay pots is that, if broken, pieces may be used for crock (see below). Disadvantages of clay pots include:
- weight—although just mentioned as an advantage, this factor does an about-turn when it comes to shifting the pots, the larger sizes are very heavy and all sizes are somewhat cumbersome to stack; • plant roots tend to stick to the sides making re-potting difficult (some pelargonium cultivars need to be repotted at least once a year—particularly for the first two or three years of growth). • Clay pots absorb the salts of fertilizers which may build up, becoming toxic to plants. • Plants need watering more often owing to porosity of clay. • Another disadvantage is that fungi and algae grow on the damp outside surface of the pot—this can be removed if desired by scrubbing or soaking in hot water (82°C (180°F)). While not detrimental to pelargonium growth, this would need to be removed to allow the plant a chance of winning a prize if exhibited on the show bench (see chapter on *Plants for Exhibition*).

Clay pots usually have one drainage hole in the middle of the bottom—this should be covered with two pieces of crock side by side over the hole (if the pieces are curved the convex part of the curve should be uppermost); over these two pieces place another piece at right angles, then cover the remaining bottom of the pot with pieces of charcoal. Charcoal is a particularly good substance to use as crock because, being porous, it absorbs moisture and nutrients (roots can often be seen clinging to pieces of charcoal). It is also useful as a soil mix ingredient (usually crushed but not to the state of being powdery), being light and helping to keep the mix porous. The size of crock should be in proportion to the size of pot, for example in a 10 cm pot use pieces about 10 mm in diameter.

Plastic Many decorator plastic pots are currently being produced in an extremely wide range of shapes, colours and sizes. One may be momentarily attracted by such pots of a bright colour; however, it is wise to consider the flower and/or leaf colour of the plant for which the pot is intended. Come winter and the fancy-leaved foliage may be overawed by a too-brightly coloured pot, and there may be a violent clash of colours when springtime flowers emerge. Depending on personal preference, the more neutral tones of white, beige, brown and green may be used to advantage in complementing the plants' own distinctive colours.

Plastic pots have the advantages of being light, easy to stack, easy to clean, and have smooth sides which plant roots do not stick to. Some have convex inner bottoms which aid drainage and make crocking unnecessary. However, if desired, pieces of charcoal or other crock may still be placed over each drainage hole.

Cement tubs, troughs and urns may also be used for growing pelargoniums. A disadvantage of this material is that it is very heavy and it would therefore be wise to consider their placement with some forethought to obviate the need to shift them. Old laundry tubs have been successfully used in this way.

Timber Left-over pieces of timber from home carpentry prove an economic way of obtaining a container to satisfy an individual requirement of shape and/or design. It is recommended that timber used in this fashion be treated to prevent the harbouring of disease organisms and rotting. Copper naphthenate, marketed by paint manufacturers, may be applied for this purpose with a paint brush. Timber window boxes are traditionally associated with the growing of zonal pelargoniums, particularly in European countries.

Wire baskets lined with bark or coconut fibre are also a popular container for pelargoniums with a trailing habit, for example, the ivy-leaved types. A disadvantage of this type of container is that it dries out very quickly, necessitating more frequent watering; in windy weather perhaps twice a day. Bark liners may be soaked until softened to facilitate moulding into wire shape.

Polystyrene This material has the advantage of being extremely lightweight, but the disadvantage of crumbling easily. When this happens, the material may be incorporated into the potting mix.

Decorative containers of china, glazed pottery and copper are also suitable for pelargonium growing.

Terrariums are not suitable because too much humidity is generated inside these containers for successful *Pelargonium* culture, the excess moisture and enclosed area creating an ideal environment for fungal and bacterial growth to thrive, both disease organisms to which pelargoniums are highly susceptible.

It will be seen from the above that there are many diverse types of containers in which pelargoniums may be grown. Choosing the right one for a particular plant in a particular situation largely remains a matter for the individual. The three most important points for growing pelargoniums in containers are: adequate sunlight, adequate air circulation and adequate drainage.

POSITIONING CONTAINERS

Naturally this will be dictated to a certain extent by geographical factors such as the layout and size of the garden or the aspect, shape and size of a home unit balcony or other location. However, the following points offer some guidelines.

Regal Pelargoniums prefer filtered sunlight or half a day of sunlight (preferably morning). While they will tolerate full sun, scorching of flowers occurs under these conditions. Regals should be protected from strong wind as they have a tendency to become top heavy with thick foliage and are easily blown over; flowers also suffer wind burn. They should be regularly checked for the presence of white fly under the leaves, aphids around new shoots and mealy bugs on leaves and stems (see *Pests, Pathogens & Problems*).

Zonal Pelargoniums will grow well in half day or full day sunlight; however, if in full sun, adequate air circulation becomes crucially important for cooling the leaves. Zonals grown against a brick wall are protected from strong wind and appreciate the warmth reflected off the bricks. Along most parts of the east coast of Australia, an east-facing wall is ideal; in areas where there are strong prevailing easterly winds, zonals may still be positioned to benefit from morning sun provided an adequate windbreak is nearby (a hedge or a man-made structure such as a timber frame covered in shadecloth for example).

Fancy-leaved zonals which are at their peak during the winter months require full sun at this time: along with cold night time temperatures, maximum foliage colouration is achieved. However, during the hot summer months, these plants should be moved to a shaded position. They will be making new growth at this time, having been pruned in spring (usually immediately after the first flush of spring flowers). They should be moved into half sun during autumn and then full sun for winter.

Dwarf and miniature zonal pelargoniums—most of these cultivars appear to do best in half day sun or filtered sunlight.

All types of zonals should be regularly inspected by looking under the leaves for rust and caterpillars.

Ivy-Leaved Pelargoniums prefer full sun: this is necessary for maximum flower production. They will grow in less than full sun, but the less sun, the less flowering will occur. The pest most likely to attack the ivy-leaves is mealy bug.

Many *Pelargonium* species may be successfully grown in pots: while the more rampant growers such as the *P. radens* syn. *P. radula* group, may be more suited to a garden (where they rapidly make a dense bush), even these, along with many of the scented species, can adapt to pot culture. They do best in filtered sun and watered only when the surface soil is quite dry. Inspect regularly for white fly.

A point which applies to all pot plants is the need to turn the pot regularly to obtain a well shaped plant. Especially if positioned against a wall, plants grow towards the light and if left unturned the foliage will all face in one direction. This, of course, may be desirable from the point of view of display; but if a particular plant is intended to be used for entry in a show, turning is an essential part of cultural preparation for such use.

POTTING THE NEWLY ROOTED CUTTING

Having successfully struck the desired cutting, it should be potted on from the rooting medium into a suitable growing medium (refer chapter on *Potting Mixtures*). The cutting should be put into a pot large enough to contain the root system and allow for some growth (a 10 cm or 12.5 cm pot is usually adequate—75 mm for miniatures). Pelargoniums have a fibrous root system (as opposed to a tap root) and therefore need to be firmed well into place when planting and protected from strong wind for a few weeks to allow the plant to consolidate. Alternatively, if troughs are the chosen containers, cuttings may be planted direct into these.

The newly potted plant should be watered immediately: this is best done by immersing the pot in water up to the height of soil level. Thus the plant is not disturbed and the medium is thoroughly soaked. To continue the preventive benefit of drenching with fungicide (as outlined in the chapter on *Propagation by Cuttings*), this first watering could also be done with a fungicide mixture.

RE-POTTING

Most pelargoniums are fast growers and may need repotting more than once per year in their early stages. (In order to avoid some of the labour involved in frequent repotting of pelargoniums, rooted cuttings may be planted straight into a larger pot than those sizes mentioned above. However, if intending to exhibit the plant, it is necessary for its size to be in proportion to the size of container.)

A plant needs repotting when the roots become a compact mass inside the container. This is evidenced by roots appearing through the drainage holes, rapid drying out of the soil and top growth out of proportion to the size of the container. The foliage may also yellow around the edges. (This latter symptom can also indicate a fertilizer deficiency or toxicity, but if recognised in conjunction with the previously mentioned symptoms of a pot-bound plant, this is more than likely an indication of this condition.) Naturally, it is desirable to repot the plant before it begins to exhibit these rather extreme symptoms. It is not difficult for those growers intimately acquainted with their plants to know when repotting is necessary. However, it is not wise to repot just as the plant is forming buds for its main spring flush of flowering. A certain amount of root disturbance always takes place when repotting and the plant should not have the added stress of re-establishing itself while it is channelling its energy into flowering. Therefore, repotting is best carried out immediately after the first main flush of spring flowers, or at pruning time in autumn. In frost-free climates, they may also be repotted throughout the winter months.

As a general rule when repotting, the roots should be disturbed as little as possible, simply adding more potting mix to the base and sides of the pot to re-settle the plant. However, if the new soil mix is of a different texture/composition/porosity to the one in the root ball, the two types should be incorporated to achieve a uniform mixture. In this instance, it would then be necessary to gently shake off the soil already around the roots.

CULTURAL REQUIREMENTS

Watering One of the most contentious aspects of the culture of any plant is 'how often should I water?' Many factors influence the watering decision: type of container, type of soil, type of plant, size of container, size of plant, the micro-climate (local climatic conditions prevailing in a particular, usually limited, area) in which the pot is situated, and so on. For pelargoniums it is better to err on the dry side than over-water, especially during humid weather. Humid damp conditions are those in which several fungal and bacterial diseases flourish: those which apply to pelargoniums are referred to in some detail in the chapter on *Pests, Pathogens & Problems*.

The ideal way to water a pot plant is to immerse it in a bucket of water as described above; however, if a great many pots are to be watered this method may prove far too time consuming. The next best method is to water the entire surface of the soil in the pot, thus ensuring that the water will penetrate all the soil in the pot. Sufficient water should be applied until it begins to run out the drainage holes. It is desirable (particularly in the case of small pots) to have a saucer or tray beneath the pot so that the water that runs out the drainage holes may be reabsorbed into the pot by capillary action: this prevents loss of nutrients which might otherwise be leached out of the soil by the constant watering required. (Capillary action in this instance applies particularly to plastic pots containing a potting mix that is not too porous.) During periods of protracted rainfall, the water should be tipped out of the trays to allow potting soil to drain. Watering should not be done again until the soil is dry at least 25 mm below the surface (even further below for larger pots). Though the surface may be very dry, a few centimetres below may still be damp and the soil in the bottom of the pot could even be in a saturated state. It is therefore necessary to probe beneath the surface. Commercial moisture meters are available which are designed to indicate the amount of moisture in the soil. It is recommended that surface soil be loosened with a fork occasionally to aerate and also to facilitate water penetration.

Fertilizing It will be appreciated that plants in containers are much more restricted in their ability to search for food via the root system than those in the ground. It is therefore necessary to supply adequate fertilizer on a regular basis. A general rule for fertilizer application is 'little and often'. This applies particularly to the use of liquid fertilizers. Too heavy a dose can cause a build-up of salts in the soil which burn the roots as the soil begins to dry out. Fertilizer application should be preceded and followed by thorough watering.

It should be noted that organic fertilizers are not effective at temperatures below 10°C. These types of fertilizers require bacterial activity to make the essential elements available to plants and bacteria are not very active in cold temperatures. If it is desired to apply fertilizer during the winter months, therefore, the use of liquid inorganic fertilizers is recommended. Also remember that application of fertilizers, over a period of time, will result in lowering the pH of the soil (increase acidity)—see below for details.

Soil Mixes The main requirements of a soil mix for pelargoniums are that it is substantial enough to support the plant (pelargoniums sometimes being inclined to be a bit wobbly owing to their fibrous root system), free draining and able to supply all the essential nutrients for normal growth. (Refer to the chapter on *Potting Mixes & Nutrients* for recommended mixtures.)

Acidity Pelargoniums grow best in a pH range of 6.5 to 7. If plants do not appear to be growing and all cultural requirements are being met, the explanation for this lack of growth may be that the soil has become too acid. When soil is too acid, the essential elements for plant growth become unavailable to the plant and it therefore becomes necessary to increase the pH to rectify this situation. The application of garden lime or dolomite will achieve this: a quantity of 2 level teaspoons per 10 cm pot is recommended.

FROST PROTECTION

Pelargoniums are easily damaged by frost; they therefore require the protection of some form of covering during winter. A glasshouse or conservatory is ideal, but failing this, almost any covering is better than none. If placed next to a house wall, the eaves may provide sufficient protection; old umbrellas may be used; a bench over the plants may be adequate. Alternatively plants may be brought indoors for the duration of frosts, provided they are positioned where they will receive the maximum amount of light, a sunroom or glass enclosed porch being suitable.

GLASSHOUSE GROWING

If desired (or necessary owing to climate), pelargoniums may be grown in the protected environment of a glasshouse. An easterly/northerly aspect is to be preferred. Shading is needed to protect the plants from afternoon sun if the temperature in the glasshouse exceeds 25°C.

Glass panels should be shaded to 50% intensity. This may be achieved by covering with shadecloth or alternatively a fibreglass roof may be substituted. It is advisable to use weldmesh (or some other type of open-weave material) for benches to avoid water build-up which creates humidity and provides a breeding ground for fungal and bacterial spores. An open-weave material also facilitates drainage. A mesh pattern measuring 75 × 50 mm is suitable for pots of 10 cm and larger. If growing miniatures, a mesh pattern of 75 × 25 mm is recommended. 75 cm is recommended as a maximum width for benches to allow access to and inspection of pots at the rear of the bench.

As mentioned elsewhere in this publication, air circulation is a prime criterion for pelargonium culture: it is therefore necessary to ensure this condition in the glasshouse, a fan shifting air at 30 m³/minute provides adequate air movement for small glasshouses and is very economical to run. Many glasshouses are fitted with louvres and/or adjustable panels to provide through ventilation.

To ensure minimal plant losses from disease, hygiene should be practised in all aspects of the culture of pelargoniums in glasshouses. The main points are to sterilize tools, disinfect benches, wash hands in disinfectant after handling diseased plant material, keep hose nozzles off the ground and avoid carrying disease organisms into glasshouses on shoes (walking over piles of soil mix on the ground for example).

It should be pointed out that pelargoniums tend to become 'leggy' more rapidly in a glasshouse or if kept too shaded than in an optimal outdoor environment: therefore regular 'pinching' of growing tips is necessary to keep the plants compact.

Also a feature of plant culture in glasshouses is the rapid multiplication of pests and spread of disease. Preventive measures should be taken at the first sign of these problems (see *Pests, Pathogens & Problems*).

Heating of the glasshouse is unnecessary unless in a climatic zone where temperatures fall below freezing point for more than a few consecutive days. Heating to maintain a minimum temperature of at least 7°C should be sufficient to tide the plants over this period. In these conditions watering should be done infrequently, let soil almost dry out between waterings and avoid splashing water onto leaves. Air circulation should still be maintained, even in these lower temperatures, to avoid freezing.

SHADEHOUSE GROWING

In temperate and warmer zones, a shadehouse is useful to protect plants from excess sun, wind and insect pests. If intending to enter plants in shows or use them for floral arrangements, it is wise to have a solid roof (PVC, fibreglass or glass (painted)) to afford protection for flowers from rain. A 28% shadecloth for walls is recommended for pelargoniums. Details of aspect, bench material and hygiene are the same as for glasshouse growing, above.

GROWING UNDER LIGHTS

It is possible to grow pelargoniums indoors under lights. Dwarf growing zonals and miniatures are more suitable than taller cultivars, for aesthetic reasons and also the fact that they are slow growers.

In order to provide sufficient light, 4 × 40 w cool white fluorescent tubes are needed for an area of 1.5 m × 0.6 m. In addition, 2 × 25 w incandescent lamps should be positioned between each set of 40 w tubes. These incandescent lamps should also be used to supplement Daylight or Deluxe cool white tubes. Alternatively Gro-Lux wide-spectrum tubes may be substituted for the above. If these are used, the 25 w incandescent lamps may be omitted. As incandescent lamps produce heat, the tops of plants need to be at least 70 cm away from the light source. With fluorescent tubes, about 30 cm is an appropriate distance.

8. GERANIUMS FOR GARDEN & LANDSCAPE

The attributes of members of the geranium family are such as to make them suitable for a wide range of situations when planning gardens and landscapes.

"Geraniums" have long been grown in Australia. One of the earliest references being in 1803 when it was recorded that: 'of the twenty-nine varieties of Forest Trees and Flowering Shrubs imported into the country, only three were "plentiful"; the sweet briar, the Provence rose, and the geranium.'

These plants finding themselves in an environment similar to that of their own, naturally flourished. The hot dry conditions and their ease of growth, together with their ability to withstand long periods of drought and still flower in abundance, soon made them a popular plant adding a radiance and perfume to their new surroundings.

The name "geranium" remained despite the reclassification as *Pelargonium* in 1789. Whatever the name, this plant became a plant of the people, a common plant, an ordinary plant, a plant that would grow well and respond with, or without care.

Increased interest over the years in other members of the Geranium Family have shown that they also have much to offer. Not so flamboyant as the popular *Pelargonium*, the *Erodium* and *Geranium* have a beauty of their own which will also enhance the garden or landscape.

Erodiums and Geraniums are ideal for rock garden landscaping (**Plate 26**). Both are relatively compact growing plants which may be used either as ground cover or as a tufted mat-forming plant. Both require well drained conditions, do well in deep soil, and are relatively free of disease and insect attack. These two genera contain well over 400 species, varieties and some cultivars. Few are illustrated in this book because of the lack of availability in Australia. Even so, some that were photographed growing in English gardens such as *Erodium supracanum* (**Plate 9**), *Erodium manescavi* (**Plate 11**), *Erodium corsicum* var. *album* (**Plate 22**) and *Geranium pylzowianum* (**Plate 12**) are worth seeking. Such plants may possibly be found in nurseries specialising in rock and alpine type garden landscaping. Failing this, Societies specialising in these plants sometimes have seed available.

The *Erodium* is most valuable for its plant form, foliage and flowers. One of the most commonly known and grown in Australia today, is the perennial *Erodium chamaedryoides* (Syn. E. reichardii) var. *roseum*. This plant becomes densely tufted forming a neat clump in the rock garden with a height of up to 15 cm (6") and a spread of about 30 cm (12"). It has small, dark green leaves which are almost completely covered in Spring with dainty pink, rounded flowers (**Plate 6**). In frost prone areas some frost protection may be required.

The annual *Erodium hymenodes*, with soft hairy foliage and covered in masses of small white to pale pink flowers in Spring and Summer (**Plate 13**) seeds readily and plants reappear each year. Effective if grown in clumps of several plants which should be removed when flowering is finished.

Erodium gruinum having larger violet blue flowers with a deeper eye, is also more effective if several plants are grown together. Its chief attribute being the remarkably long-beaked fruit which clearly demonstrates the seed dispersal technique described in another chapter.

Erodium crinitum, an Australian native *Erodium* has a propensity to take over under good growing conditions, therefore should be planted where it can spread far and wide. Seeding freely, once established it will come again and again. For the collector however, it is worthy of attention if only for the tiny intense blue flowers which clearly show the yellow stamens.

Plants in the genus *Geranium* are more widely grown and may be found in many rock and alpine type gardens. Ideally suited for this type of gardening, they may also be used in the open garden where they combine well as a border plant with other perennials.

There are some annual forms which are interesting plants to grow in the home garden. They are all introduced species which seed freely, and yet each has something different to offer and are commonly grown in Australia.

Geranium molle with its rounded leaves and ground cover plant form, has many small pale pink flowers in Spring and early Summer. Grows well in paths and driveways covering the soil and helping to prevent weed growth.

Geranium robertianum ("Herb Robert") has dainty fern-like foliage and small mauve-purple flowers. It is prized for the beautiful red colouring of the foliage in autumn and winter. Upright growing, an individual plant makes a delightful pot plant, or several growing in the garden give a drift of soft foliage to the landscape. Naturalizes easily.

Geranium nepalense forms a dense spreading plant up to 60 cm and a height of about 15 to 20 cm (6″–8″). Leaves are dark green, nicely lobed and bright purple flowers are produced in abundance in late Autumn when the other species have finished.

The perennial types respond well to cooler, mountain gardens although many are grown in Sydney suburban areas.

Geranium sanguineum ("Bloody crane's bill") has large crimson to blood-red flowers about 3 cm (1½″) across and is a good ground cover. Growth spread approximately 60 cm (2′) with a height of about 25 cm (10″). There are also forms which come in white, pale pink and reddish-purple flower colourings.

Geranium pratense ('Meadow cranes bill') with its large violet-blue flowers is a native of England and Northern Europe (**Plate** 7). It prefers moist grassy places and in some areas the foliage takes on interesting autumn tints. Forming leafy clumps it grows to about 60 cm in height with a spread of about 30 cm (12″). There are also double forms but it is doubtful that these are available in Australia (**Plate 7**).

Geranium phaeum ("Mourning Widow") or ("Dusky cranes bill"). This plant has deep purple almost black flowers with reflexed petals. Does well in shady places, naturalizing well and forming into tough clumps about 60 cm in height, spread about 30 cm (12″).

Geranium renardii has velvety grey-green foliage and white flowers veined with blackish purple. Does best in sunny positions with dappled shade, forming neat hummocks about 25 cm (10″) high (**Plate 8**).

Geranium dalmaticum forms neat hummocks also, has rounded shiny leaves and grows to an approximate height of 22 cm (9″). Flowers are clear pink and held well above the foliage (**Plate 10**). Seems to prefer poor soil and dappled sun.

Geranium incanum an ideal plant for general garden planting or in the rock garden. A South African species it revels in the Australian sunshine and is quite different in appearance from the plants already described and which come from the Northern Hemisphere. The foliage is finely cut and fern like, tending to spread with thin branching stems covering the ground for up to almost a metre in width. Growing to a height of about 30 cm (12″) it is a haze of blue, almost cornflower blue, in Spring and Summer. Also can be grown as a hanging basket specimen.

The popular *Pelargonium* has many uses in the garden and landscape particularly where bright, long sustained colour is required. With its natural ability to withstand long periods of drought in the open garden it is a popular choice where a plant requiring little attention is needed. Its chief requirements are a warm sunny position, a friable soil with a pH reading of 6.5 to 7, good drainage, and an occasional application of a balanced fertilizer, (see chapter on *Potting Mixes & Nutrients*).

These plants may be affected by frosts so need protection in frost prone areas, or alternatively they may be planted out as Spring and Summer plants and removed during Autumn and Winter as is done in many countries overseas.

Whilst garden planning and landscape design has changed over the years, particularly in the field of town planning, community and civic projects, the average home gardener still tends to create an atmosphere of a more intimate nature, reflecting their personality and life style, yet in keeping with the overall concept of environmental and climatic conditions.

In large cities the trend to concentrated living means that more emphasis is placed on container grown plants for patio, terrace or courtyard, and even in plazas and shopping centres. Care is specially needed here in the choice of position, plant and container. Each should complement the other and blend into the surrounding landscape.

Within *Pelargonium* there are four major groups which may be used effectively both in the home garden and the landscape. These are the ZONAL, IVY-LEAVED, REGAL and SCENTED-LEAVED Pelargoniums.

Suggested areas where these may be used to good effect are given and later suitable cultivars recommended. The choice of complementary or contrasting colour combinations is a personal one, depending to a large extent on the given environment and the general effect to be created.

In large scale landscaping such as industrial and shopping complexes, city plazas and window boxes, the zonal or ivy-leaved pelargonium may be used. In massed bedding displays or in large tubs and urns these plants are also effective. The ivy-leaved pelargonium is ideal for ground cover either on flat or sloping sites in the landscape or even along the embankments of roadways. It should be noted that where the ivy-leaved plants are used for ground cover there may be need to provide some form of soil control such as wire mesh if the slope of the ground warrants it. Otherwise soil erosion may occur. These adaptable plants will, with support, also cover unsightly stumps or fences.

The regal *Pelargonium*, on the other hand, being essentially a Spring and Summer flowering plant needs to be planted where there are other plants to take over when the regals have finished flowering. Mostly tall, upright growing, they challenge the Azalea for abundance of flowers and brilliance of colour. A planting of regal pelargoniums facing North in the Eastern states, carefully planned in early, mid and late flowering cultivars, will flower in conjunction with Azaleas and will continue on well after they have finished.

The scented-leaved *Pelargonium* is most useful in areas of some shade and beside much used pathways where they may be brushed against to release the scent. A wide range of leaf shapes, growth habits and perfumes make these a valuable addition to any garden. Much pleasure has been given when these plants have been used in gardens for the blind or other disabled persons, where they add a fragrance that is both tantalizing and appealing. Some guidance is needed in planning such a pathway or garden for many of these plants grow rapidly and have a tendency to take over from the more slow growing, compact forms.

Some suggested plants for specific purposes.

Massed Bedding (Plate 55)

'Dark Red Irene' or any of the 'Irene' group for strong, continuing colour. Height to about 60 cm (2′), spread about 25 cm (10″). The 'Irene' group comes in a wide colour range, from white, through pink, salmon, orange-red to brilliant scarlet.

'Orange Ricard'; 'Lavender Ricard' or any of the strong growing French or Bruant strain. Growth similar to the 'Irene' group, they also come in a wide colour range.

'Deacon Mandarin'; 'Deacon Fireball' or any of the 'Deacon' group for low compact growing plants with an abundance of flowers. Height and spread to about 25 cm (10″). Wide colour range from white, through light pink to lilac, salmon, orange and scarlet.

Border Planting

'Leonie Holborow' or any of the 'Black Opal' group (**Plate 40**). Dark purple to almost black leaved dwarf zonal pelargoniums which cover themselves with flower for many months of the year. Height to approximately 30 cm and spread to 25 cm (10″).

'Madame Salleron' a compact growing dwarf plant having green leaves edged with creamy/white. Does not flower but produces a good effect with foliage as a border plant. Height to about 20 cm (8″) and spread about 30 cm (12″) (**Plate 30**).

'Sun Rocket' a dwarf growing plant with yellow-green foliage, and bright orange flowers. Compact growth to about 25 cm (10″). Other dwarf growing zonals which may also be used for border planting are 'Black Vesuvius', 'Bird Dancer' etc.

'Antoine Crozy' ('Pierre Crozy'; 'Scarlet Bedder') is the plant which has become known as the "common red geranium". Found growing in many Australian gardens it has and still does, provide a wealth of colour. Bright orange-scarlet flowers, self branching growth, it attains a height of anything from 30 cm (12″) to 60 cm (2′) depending on growing conditions and position. Often used as a border outside the fence of a suburban or country home. Rust resistant (**Plate 31**).

Rock Garden Planting

As well as the *Geranium* and *Erodium* species mentioned earlier in this chapter, many dwarf and miniature zonal pelargoniums do well also in this type of garden landscaping. The truly compact growing plants such as 'Cecilie' or 'Nyndee Too' are ideal as are also the 'Black Opal' group and the two miniature ivy-leaved plants 'Gay Baby' and 'Sugar Baby'.

Planting of a rock garden needs careful planning as to times of flowering, colour of flowers and/or foliage, together with height and spread of the plants to be used. Maintenance, once planted, is also required such as the removal of dead flower heads from time to time. Pruning and shaping of pelargoniums should be carried out each autumn and *Geranium* and *Erodium* plants divided every two or three years depending on their growth.

Window Box Planting

Window boxes should be of simple design, well constructed and practical to use. Not too small, with a suggested length of one to 1.3 metres (4′-4′6″). Top width should be at least 30 cm (12″), bottom width 23 cm (9″) and a depth of about 20 cm (8″). Many window boxes do not give adequate depths of soil for plants growing usually in warm sunny positions, so the depth of 20 cm is recommended or even deeper if the position will allow it.

Plants suitable for growing in these boxes include many of the flowering zonal pelargoniums, particularly the strong growing French or Bruant types. Any of the hybrid ivy-leaved pelargoniums or any of the ivy-leaved depending on the positioning of the box, may also be used.

Hybrid ivy-leaved plants and the more compact growing ivy-leaved, being rust resistant may be preferable for boxes that are fairly inaccessible for regular maintenance.

Suggested plants for these boxes are the hybrid ivy-leaved pelargoniums such as 'Antoine Crozy', 'Millfield Gem', 'Achievement', 'Schöne Schwarzwälderin' and the beautiful 'Blauer Fruhling'.

For window boxes with a short drop, the short noded, more compact growing ivy-leaved pelargoniums such as 'Galilee', 'Her Majesty the Queen', 'Santa Paula' or 'Mrs Perrin' are suggested. For those boxes with a longer drop, such as on large city buildings, longer trailing types such as 'Intensity', 'Madame Crousse', and 'Mexican Beauty' may be used.

Ground Cover (Plates 29 and 69)

The short jointed, compact growing, flowering ivy-leaved pelargoniums mentioned above make good ground cover plants. The two miniature ivy-leaved pelargoniums 'Sugar Baby' and 'Gay Baby' are ideal although the latter has a limited flowering season.

Care should be taken in the early growing of any of these plants to ensure that compact, close foliaged plants are formed before flowering commences. Other ground cover plants include the *Geranium* species mentioned earlier in this chapter.

Spillovers and Climbers (Plate 28)

Again the ivy-leaved pelargoniums are a choice for this purpose. Fast growing, long trailing plants such as mentioned above are ideal. They will cover well in a short period of time and only require attention to pruning procedures each year to maintain compact cover (see *Pruning & Shaping*).

Tubs, Urns and other Containers

The size of the container will determine the plant or plants best suited to it in proportion to both the container and the surroundings. The location with regard to sun and shade also being important. In areas such as plazas and city squares, provided the location is suitable, tall growing zonal pelargoniums, grouped together for quick fill, may be used to advantage. Where Spring and early Summer flowering only is needed the regal pelargonium could be most effective. Some compact growing ivy-leaved pelargoniums may also be used to spill over the sides softening the appearance of the container.

Many other unusual containers may be used, creating interest and colour in the landscape as will be seen in **Plates 27 and 32**.

Standard Plants

The art of growing pelargoniums as standards has long been practised overseas but little used in Australia. Perhaps the illustration of the standard regal (**Plate 36**) will inspire growers to attempt to achieve this effect for accent on patio or terrace.

To grow such a plant a two year period may be required. The first year in shaping and training the plant with some flowers being achieved. The second year the basic structure will be there so the effect as seen in the illustration should be possible. Strong growing ivy-leaved and zonal pelargoniums may also be used for this purpose.

Decorative Work

Another aspect of the *Pelargonium*, outside the scope of this book, and yet one which should not be overlooked, is its suitability as cut material for decorative work.

Beautiful flower and foliage arrangements (**Plates 4, 56 and 95**), massed brilliant colour in a basket (**Plate 96**) "Old World" posies or other "Make Up" work are just a few of the many interesting and delightful uses of the versatile *Pelargonium*.

Special Places for Special Plants

The unusual and weird *Pelargonium* species may well be a focal interest point in the landscape where an arid, stony cactus type garden can be established. In fact many succulent pelargoniums are grown by Cacti enthusiasts. It is in this setting of sunny, well drained pebble gardens that these plants are shown to best advantage.

Plants suitable include *Pelargonium echinatum, Pelargonium gibbosum, Pelargonium carnosum* and *Pelargonium tetragonum*.

These plants need little care, being best left to grow in their own natural habit, remembering that when they are dormant little or no watering is required, their total needs being supplied by rain.

GERANIACEAE, this plant family with such variation and diversity must surely have something to offer to all people, in all places, and in all seasons. The more knowledge of, and the longer the acquaintance with the family, the greater the fascination will become, and it may well be that it will be classed as the most desirable plant family for contemporary landscaping.

9. SELECTED PELARGONIUM CULTIVARS & SPECIES

The number of *Pelargonium* cultivars and species is so great that it is only possible to present a representative list within the scope of this book.

A complete list of all known *Pelargonium* cultivar names is being compiled by the Australian Geranium Society as International Registration Authority for *Pelargonium*. Some parts of this List are already available from that Society.

In compiling the list of plants described here an attempt has been made to cover those plants which may be recommended, either for general garden use, container growing or as cut material for floral work. Many of the plants described are also illustrated which should assist in easy identification and enable the reader to choose a plant to suit personal taste or for a particular purpose.

In this list the abbreviation Rg followed by a number and immediately following the cultivar name, indicates that such name has been registered with the International Registration Authority for *Pelargonium* and is therefore not available for re-use in any section of genus *Pelargonium*.

In describing the colour of a flower consideration is given for personal differences in colour recognition. Many descriptions are given in general colour terms only, such as rose-red, orange-scarlet etc., others have also been colour charted. The colour chart used is The Royal Horticultural Society's Colour Chart, 1966, and abbreviated to RHSCC in the text.

It must be appreciated that colour charting is only a guide and should not be considered sufficient evidence, on its own, for identification. Climatic conditions, cultural procedures, the condition or age of the bloom when charted, all contribute to possible colour variation.

Where there is a bracketed name following a cultivar name, it will either be a synonym, a misrepresented spelling of the name or a popular descriptive name applied to that plant.

It is to be noted that recommendations given for the use of these plants is for frost free areas. In frost prone areas some form of protection will be required.

Flowering Zonal Pelargoniums

'**Always**' Double creamy-white, flushed soft salmon, darker in the centre and sometimes at the margins. Large flowers of good form freely produced on a medium sized bushy plant. Excellent for container growing. If grown in the open garden some light shade during summer may be necessary. A similar plant is 'Anne Richards', same type flower, slightly more cream with deeper flushing in the centre.

'**Annette Both**' Single pale orchid-pink to lavender-mauve, with narrow petals slightly furled. Attractive dark, crinkled foliage on a miniature sized plant. Excellent for container growing.

'**Apple Blossom Rosebud**' Double white with distinct rose-red edging to the petals and sometimes light green in centre of flower. Very double flowers in the form of a tiny half opened rosebud. Upright growth. Excellent for container growing or a garden specimen. Also useful as cut material for posies and floral arrangements (**Plate 16** and **99**).

'**Ashley Irene**' Semi-double flowers of an unusual soft scarlet, RHSCC 43C. Five to seven petals per floret with some petaloids. Upper petals flushed RHSCC 43D. Reverse of petals have white overcast. Typical 'Irene' type leaf with irregular dark green zoning. Strong upright growth. Good garden plant or large container.

'**Betty Fitzell**' Single flowers, magenta with a touch of orange on the upper petals. Deep green leaves, zoned. Dwarf growth. Excellent plant for container growing.

'**Blossomtime**' Semi-double flowers, soft salmon coral RHSCC 68B (nearest). An unusual and distinctive colour. Dark green leaves with broad, deeper green zone. Strong, bushy upright growth. Good garden plant or large container.

'**Charles Gounoud**' ('**Charles Gounod**') Large double flowers white edged and flushed magenta through to deep magenta RHSCC 66A. Reverse of petals white flushed RHSCC 57B-61B. Free flowering on medium stems. Distinctive and effective. Growth vigorous and strong. Sometimes known as 'Madame Guinier'. Good garden plant or large container.

'**Deacon Romance**' Double flowers of neon pink. The "Deacons" are a group of plants often called "Floribunda pelargoniums" because of their propensity for prolonged and abundant flowering. Compact, dwarf growing plants producing many heads of flowers over a long period they are ideal for border planting or container growing. Other "Deacons" include 'Deacon Barbecue' Bright pink; 'Deacon Coral Reef' coral pink;

'Deacon Fireball' scarlet; and 'Deacon Lilac Mist' pale lilac. There are several others including the recent novelty 'Deacon Peacock' with double orange-red flowers and leaves of dark green with splashes of apple green inside an irregular reddish-brown zone. 'Deacon Romance' (**Plate 38**)

'**Debutante**' Large semi-double soft salmon-pink RHSCC 49A flushed and veined 43D. Small white eye, prominent stamens. Mid-green leaves, deeper green at outer edges. Vigorous, upright strong growth. Large container plant or open garden. There is also a regal pelargonium by this name.

'**Emma Hossler**' Double light rose pink, white centre. A free flowering semi-dwarf hardy plant excellent plant for container growing or border planting. Others of this type are 'Mr Everaarts' deep pink, 'Tu-Tone' varying shades of light and dark pink and 'Dick's White' ('Blanchette').

'**Encore**' Semi-double coral-apricot RHSCC 43C/B, with light eye and light reverse to petals. Large cup-shaped flowers with five to six petals and some petaloids, upper petals lightly flushed and feathered. Leaves are pale green with faint zone. A strong growing plant for garden or large container (**Plate 43**).

'**Eric Hoskins' Rg 1** Double pale pink to deep salmon in centre of flower. In cooler weather shading to deep salmon-orange. In warmer weather bloom has a silver sheen. A beautiful combination of colours in extremely large rounded heads of flowers. Leaves distinctly zoned. Plant compact and dwarf growing. A similar plant but with slightly deeper coloured flowers is 'Silberlachs'.

'**Exquisite Elf**' (formerly No 471) Single, white flowers of typical five-fingered form. Petals turn pink on the edges and bottom petals flush pink, as the blooms age. Leaves five-fingered in form, light green with darker green borders. Strong, upright growth. Flowers produced in abundance over a long period. Garden or large container.

'**Francis Parrett**' Double, bright fuchsine pink, rosette type flowers in tight clusters, RHSCC 67C (nearest). Dark green leaves. Compact miniature growth. Excellent container plant.

'**Freckles**' Semi-double pearly white generously speckled with crimson spots. Large blooms on a medium sized head. Leaves light green without zone. Compact growth, but not vigorous. One of the Bird's Egg group, others include 'Double Pink Bird's Egg'; 'Plenty' and the singles 'Margaret Kay' and 'Tobruk'. Good container plants.

'**Grannie Hewitt**' ('**Pigmy**') Double scarlet RHSCC 43B, centre petals lightly touched carmine. Small flowers on slender erect stems above tiny green leaves with a very faint zone. Miniature to dwarf growing making an excellent small container plant (**Plate 41**).

'**Inspiration**' Semi-double creamy white to pale salmon flowers, buds soft apricot-salmon before opening. Extremely large cup-shaped flowers freely produced on a strong growing French type plant. Medium sized and bushy. Container or garden (**Plate 33**).

'**Irene**' Semi-double bright red to clear crimson. There is a large group of plants known as the "Irenes" all with large semi-double flowers produced freely and strong growing habit. Leaf growth is large, slightly downy in texture and usually zoned with slightly darker green. Many are available including 'Dark Red Irene'; 'Salmon Irene'; 'Toyon'; 'Party Dress'; 'Ashley Irene' and 'Modesty'. Good for large containers and tubs, garden bedding or window box.

'**Irma**' Double salmon-apricot RHSCC 41C (nearest), lower petals porcelain rose RHSCC 43D (nearest), white centre. Sparse truss, on slender stems. Leaves small, fleshy, showing apparent

relationship to the species *Pelargonium acetosum*. Upright growth. An interesting and unusual container plant.

'**Lady of Spain**' Single soft coral-pink, large white eye. RHSCC 52D, veined 52C. Flowers and flower head large. Free flowering, tall growing plant. A similar flower but softer in colour is 'Moonmist'. Container or garden.

'**Lavender Ricard**' Semi-double lavender-rose with white centre. Large heads of flower on a tall growing strong plant. Free blooming French type, others of which are 'Alphonse Ricard' and 'Orange Ricard'. 'Lavender Ricard' (**Plate 44**). Large container, bedding or window box.

'**Little Primula**' Single off-white shaded pale rose pink, distinctive phlox-eye type centre to floret RHSCC 52D. Small dark green leaves without zone. Dwarf compact habit with blooms held well above the foliage. Container or garden.

'**Lullaby**' Double soft salmon sometimes with lighter margins. The colour varies with cultural conditions. Large full flowers on a bushy medium sized plant. Excellent for container growing, needs attention to feeding and watering. When grown in the garden needs some shade from hot summer sun. Other similar plants include 'A.E. Bond'; 'Cameo'; 'Tresor'; 'Tintinbar' and 'Dagmar Murray'. Each varying slightly in colour combinations. All excellent container plants.

'**Magnificent**' Semi-double, rich light salmon-pink. Enormous flowers on a large strong growing plant. Flower colour is slightly deeper than 'Fiat Enchantress'. A good garden subject or large container. Needs some attention to feeding and watering during long flowering periods. Other similar plant is 'Nimbus' white, flushed salmon. 'Magnificent' (**Plate 39**)

'**Maxim Kovalevski**' Single brilliant orange flowers of good size and shape. RHSCC 40A/B. Soft green leaves without zone. Plant of medium dwarf habit and slender stems. Free flowering. Good for garden bedding or container growing. Other single orange types are 'Golden Lion' and 'Janet Scott'.

'**Mellinda**' Single white, light magenta centre. Flower petals of thin texture, edges slightly wavy, faintly edged light magenta. Leaves deep soft green, with downy texture. Dwarf to semi-dwarf growth. Good container plant or garden specimen.

'**Monsieur Emile David**' Semi-double purple RHSCC 67B, with a white centre. Large flowers on long stems held well above the foliage. Strong, vigorous growing plant. Large container, tub or urn, or garden bedding. Other plants in this group are 'Olympia' and 'Dagata'.

'**Mrs Lawrance**' ('**Mrs M.A. Lawrance**') Double soft oyster pink, flushed deeper to centre and lighter on edges. Large flowers opening flat, produced in medium sized heads on a dwarf to medium growing plant. Excellent container plant or open garden in protected position. Two sports from this plant are 'Mrs G. Clark' with white stems and butterfly-zoned leaves and 'Retah's Crystal' a silver leaved sport from 'Mrs G. Clark'. All make good container plants.

'**Mrs Tarrant**' Double white, edged and flushed rose-pink. Small flowers on medium sized heads, produced freely. Zoned foliage, dwarf branching habit of growth. Excellent container or garden plant (**Plate 45**).

'**Mr Wren**' Single light red flowers with a conspicuous white edge. A distinct novelty. Tall growing, needs attention to shaping. For best results grow a little dry toward flowering time. Will sometimes revert to a plain all red form.

'**Multicolour**' Single pale pink deepening to deep rose as the blooms age. Both colours show on the plant at the same time. Effective on a small, compact growing plant. Good container or garden specimen (**Plate 14**).

'New Life' One of a group of zonal pelargoniums all related in some way to the old variety 'Vesuvius'. 'New Life', a sport of the scarlet 'Vesuvius' has single rounded flowers striped red and white. It will sometimes revert to the original parent, or produce a sport known as 'Phlox New Life'. 'Phlox New Life' has single rounded flowers of white slightly flushed pink with a coral pink centre or eye. 'Double New Life' a sport from 'Wonderful' (a double form of 'Vesuvius') is also striped red and white. All free flowers, compact growing plants suitable for container growing.

'Orion' Double orange-red. The extremely double flowers are produced in abundance on a short bushy, compact growing plant. Dark leaves with some zoning. This plant is one of the parents of the 'Deacon' group (**Plate 19**).

'Paris' Single white, fine red edge to all petals. Tall growing, strong plant carrying large heads of blooms of perfect form, held well above the foliage. A similar plant is 'Joan's Choice'.

'Phlox Eye' Single white, flushed pink, with deeper pink centre. Tall growing leggy plant which needs shaping in the garden. The name 'Phlox Eye' is more commonly used to describe a group of plants all having a centre to the flower of a darker colour. Many combinations are available. One such is 'Phlox New Life', a sport of 'New Life'. 'Phlox Eye' (**Plate 15**)

'Pink Cloud' Semi-double light salmon pink. Free blooming. Large strong plant, fast growing and bred to withstand summer heat it can be recommended for garden planting in warmer areas.

'Pink Poinsettia' Double rose-pink quilled type flower, a few petals showing some white near the base of the flower. Medium growth, an excellent container plant. Other quilled types include 'Alfred Zitzer' crimson, 'Noel' white and 'Spitfire'. 'Pink Poinsettia' (**Plate 18**)

'Prince of Wales' Single flowers tyrian purple RHSCC 57A (nearest), flushed darker. Upper petals distinctly based orange/red RHSCC 43B (nearest). An old variety, free flowering, well known and popular. Good garden plant or container if shaped.

'Princess Fiat' Semi-double to double white, lightly flushed salmon. Flowers are exquisite, having serrated petals and giving the impression of a carnation. A small, compact free blooming plant ideal for container growing. Other "Fiats" include 'Royal Fiat', 'Fiat Queen', 'Fiat Supreme' and 'Fiat King'. Attention is needed to remove any growth having flowers reverting to a plain flowered form.

'Red Demon' Single scarlet, typical petal formation of the five-fingered group. Leaves five-fingered form and growth similar to the parent 'Chinese Cactus-Fiery Chief'. Many plants have been bred from the original parent and are known as "The Staphs", "Stellars" or the "Five-fingered" group. Container or garden. 'Red Demon' (**Plate 17**).

'Skelly's Pride' ('Jeanne') Single azalea pink RHSCC 41C, crenate petals. Small heads of medium sized flowers held well above the foliage. Free flowering. Leaves slightly smooth. Medium growing plant. Sometimes it will revert to its plain flowered parent 'Flame'. There is also a pink form 'Pink Skelly's' ('Sweet William') and a sport from 'Skelly's Pride' known as 'Deep Skelly's'. Container or garden. 'Skelly's Pride' (**Plate 20**)

'Wedding Day' Rg 18 Double, pure white. Flowers of perfect form in large heads on a strong growing plant. Does not 'pink' with age. Good container plant or garden specimen (**Plate 42**).

'Xenia Field' Single white, veined and flushed to RHSCC 43B in centre. Centre of flower appears deep rose-red. Medium sized flowers held well above the foliage on a medium growing plant. Leaves unzoned. Garden or container (**Plate 34**).

Fancy-Leaved Zonal Pelargoniums

'Alfred Holmes' Rg 31 Golden green leaves, bronze zone, colour deepens in Winter. Double scarlet flowers RHSCC 43A deepening with age to 45B, many petalled. Trusses large and rounded, held on tall stems above the foliage. Growth stocky, short jointed. Good container plant.

'Ann Tilling' Golden green leaves with bronze zone, deepening in winter. Small, single salmon-red flowers RHSCC 47D, on slender stems held well above the foliage. Tall growing, bushy branching habit. Rust resistant. Good garden subject particularly if planted against a wall. Excellent as cut material for floral work during winter.

'Argyle' Rg 49 Golden green leaves, bronze zone, deepening in Winter. Single white flowers lightly flushed pink. Tightly formed truss held well above the foliage on erect stems. Strong growth to 30.4 cm (12″). Flowers well, particularly in Spring. Good container plant.

'Bird Dancer' Dark green leaves heavily zoned black on outer edge. Typical five-fingered form. In colder weather leaves appear almost black. Single salmon-pink flowers, upper petals RHSCC 52C, lower 52D. All petals narrow, top two thinner than bottom three. Dwarf growth with a profusion of flowers held well above the foliage. Other plants of this type are 'Flamingo Dancer' and 'Devil Dancer'. Two miniature forms are 'Bon Bon' and 'Bijou'. All make excellent container plants.

'Black Opal' A group of four plants each having single flowers, and dark foliage. 'Black Opal' No 1, dark leaf deepening to black, with shaded centre zone. Flowers single salmon-pink RHSCC 38D deepening with age to 38A. 'Black Opal' No 2, almost black leaf, narrow zone, midway on leaf. Flowers soft pink RHSCC 52D. 'Black Opal' No 3, very dark leaf, darker to the outer edge in a broad zone. Flowers very pale pink, veined. 'Black Opal' No 4. Flowers light pink almost cream, smaller than No 3. Dark leaf pencilled narrow zone midway on leaf. All are very floriferous. 'Black Opal' No 1 dwarf to semi-dwarf growth, the other three miniature to dwarf spreading growth, which makes them ideal rock garden plants or useful for bordering a garden. Also good as container plants (**Plate 40**).

'Chelsea Gem' ('Mrs Churchill', 'Lady Churchill') Leaves green edged white. Flowers double fuchsine pink RHSCC 62B/C (nearest), paling in centre, white base to upper petals. Free flowering. Medium sized flowers and head. Growth dwarf and shrubby. A similar plant with which it is sometimes confused is 'Mrs Parker' double deeper pink. 'Caroline Schmidt' has similar foliage and growth semi-dwarf. Flowers double blood red. All make good garden or container plants (**Plate 51**).

'Corroboree' Dark green leaf with centre black zone. During winter leaves shade bronze and green, with a fine cream edge. Rounded leaves, slightly crinkled. Single salmon-red flowers. Strong branching habit, slightly spreading. Good as cut material for decorative work. Others in this group are 'Walkabout', 'Munjon', 'Playtime' and 'Nimitybel'. All hardy garden plants.

'Crystal Palace Gem' Yellow-green leaf with distinct butterfly marking in dark green showing clearly in centre of leaf. Small single rose-red flowers. Dwarf, well branched habit. Sometimes confused with 'Mangle's Variegated' with similarly coloured and marked leaves of a thinner, smoother texture and single bright red flowers (**Plate 58**).

'Distinction' ("One-in-a-ring") Dark green leaves, distinct black, narrowly pencilled zone, running evenly around the leaf near the outer margin. Tightly formed flower heads of single orient red RHSCC 45B (nearest) flushed rose madder at the throat. Slender erect dwarf growth.

'Dolly Varden' ('Dolly Vardon') Silver tri-colour having a green leaf with slight white edge, broad brown-purple zone touched carmine near the centre. Single small red flowers RHSCC 43A. Dwarf to medium habit. 'Miss Farren' is similar but taller growing. An Australian form, known as South Australian 'Dolly Vardon' is an improved form of the original, having a wider cream-white leaf edge and more intense markings (Plate 54).

'Fairyland' Silver tri-colour. Leaves grey-green, pale ivory border, zoned with irregular splashes of rose-red. In cold weather the border becomes pink to rose-red and the zone deepens in colour. Small single scarlet flowers Small leaves on a miniature, slow growing, very bushy, spreading plant. Does best in 70mm (3") pots. A true collector's plant. Similar highly coloured, slow growing plants for the collector include 'Elf', 'Sprite, and 'Blazonry'. (Plate 52)

'Flower of Spring' Green leaves edged creamy white. Small single vermilion flowers RHSCC 40A. Medium, upright growth, sparse flowering. Good bedding plant. Others similar are 'Grey Monk', 'Attraction' and 'Kathleen Harrop'.

'Frank Headley' Green leaves edged creamy-white border of varying width around a centre butterfly zone of green. Single dawn pink flowers RHSCC 43D (nearest). Dwarf, upright growth. Free flowering. Good container plant.

'Freak of Nature' Green leaves, large centre blotch of creamy-white almost covering the leaf. Small single vermilion flowers RHSCC 41B/A. Dwarf, slow growing plant difficult to maintain with good centre blotching. Stems having leaves reverting to green should be removed. A collector's plant. (Plate 35)

'Gold Coast' Yellow gold leaves showing faint buff zone in Winter, little or no zone in Summer. Leaves slightly hairy. Flowers single pink with deeper pink phlox-eye type centre. Strong, upright growth. Good garden plant.

'Golden Harry Hieover' ('Alpha') Yellow-green glossy leaves, with distinct chestnut zone. Small single vermilion flowers RHSCC 41A, in sparse heads. Thin stemmed, lax, dwarf growth. A good border or rock garden plant. There is also a pink flowered form 'Pink Harry Hieover'. Rust prone.

'Golden Staph' Golden leaves, slight bronze zone more clearly marked in winter. Typical five-fingered leaf and flower form. Single pale vermilion flowers, two upper petals narrow and three lower much broader, white at base. Container or garden.

'Happy Thought' Green leaves with centre butterfly zone of gold or ivory, sometimes showing reddish zone on younger leaves in cold weather. Reverse colourings of 'Crystal Palace Gem'. Small single flowers crimson-red. Medium growth, erect stems. There is a pink flowering form 'Pink Happy Thought' with similar leaf colouring but more lax in growth habit. Container or garden.

'Hills of Snow' Grey-green leaves edged creamy-white. Single flowers pale mauve-pink. Upright semi-dwarf habit. Garden or container. A similar combination of leaf and flower colour is found in 'Petals'.

'Jubilee' Golden green leaf, broad chestnut zone almost to edge of leaf. Single salmon-pink flowers. Strong growing, tall upright plant. Good garden plant.

'Kelly Anne' Yellow green leaves with irregular reddish zone, deepening in Winter. Scalloped edges to leaf. Large single flowers deep salmon RHSCC 44D (nearest), top petals flushed 44C toward small white throat. Tall upright growth, needs shaping to produce a good plant. Garden or container.

'Lass O'Gowrie' ('Carse O'Gowrie') Silver tri-colour. Grey-green leaves, narrow cream edging and purple-brown zone

splashed rose-red. Single red flowers RHSCC 43A. Dwarf growth. Not as colourful as 'Miss Burdett Coutts' but easier to grow. Container plant. (Plate 53)

'Leonie Holborow' Deep purple-black glossy leaves, very dark zone. In winter leaves almost black. Single salmon flowers RHSCC 41C deepening to 41B. Flowers are produced in abundance over a long period. Excellent plant for rock garden, border or container. Dwarf branched growth sometimes growing to 30 cm (12") or more in good conditions.

'Lively Lady' Pale golden-green leaves, unzoned, and of a delicate texture. Single orange-scarlet flowers with small white eye. A bushy, compact dwarf growing plant. Container plant.

'Lynbrook Silver' Rg 114 Lemon-gold leaves, lightly zoned deeper. Colour intensifies in winter. Leaf and flower typical five-fingered form. Flowers single pure white, medium sized truss on medium length stems. Slow growing plant to 30.4 cm (12") in height and approximately the same in width. Prolific bloomer. Excellent container and show plant.

'Madame Butterfly' Olive green leaf, ivory white edge and green butterfly zone in centre. Double currant red flowers, RHSCC 45D/C. Dwarf growth. Container plant.

'Madame Salleron' ('Mme Salleron') Green leaves irregularly bordered creamy-white. A compact growing, tufted plant forming large clumps to 30 cm (12") and about 20 cm (8") high. Does not flower in the variegated form. May be propagated by division. Excellent border plant or rock garden specimen. A taller growing silver leaved form with single carmine-rose, small flowers is 'Little Trot'. ('Madame Salleron' Plate 30).

'Magic Lantern' Green leaves variously splashed red, yellow and bright green. Rust coloured zone and pale green butterfly marking. Single salmon-red flowers. Strong growing with slight trailing habit. Good hanging basket subject. 'Mosaic' a similar plant has slightly more upright growth. Garden or container.

'Masterpiece' Green-gold leaves with bronze zone clearly defined. Young leaves show better colour having a more golden leaf with a more reddish zone. Small, double camellia rose flowers held well above the foliage. RHSCC 52C (nearest), deepening with age. Slow growing, compact dwarf habit. Good container plant. (Plate 57)

'Medallion' Yellow to yellow-green leaves with large red-brown blotches filling the centre of the leaf. Small, single dark salmon flowers borne in profusion. Habit of growth bushy and spreading. Good for hanging baskets or containers. (Plate 50)

'Mr Henry Cox' ('Mrs Henry Cox') Golden tri-colour. Leaves, outer border citron green, shadow zone, varying in depth, of colour mandarin-red, irregular darker zone from ivy green to almost black. Single begonia pink RHSCC 48D deepening in centre. Brilliantly coloured foliage on an upright growing semi-dwarf plant. Colour intensity increases in cold weather. Good container or garden plant. A similarly coloured plant, although not so intensely, is 'Lady Cullum' with single red flowers. ('Mr Henry Cox' Plate 48)

'Mrs Strang' ('Double Mrs Pollock') Golden tri-colour. Leaves variously marked with green, zoned mandarin red, irregular bright yellow border. In cold weather leaves are brightly marked scarlet, crimson and brown. Small double vermilion red flowers. Sturdy, medium sized plant. Other similar golden tri-colours are 'Mrs Pollock' single flowers, 'Contrast' and 'Peter Grieve'. Good container plants. 'Mrs Pollock' and 'Mrs Strang' make good garden plants for winter colour. (Plate 47)

'Nyndee Too' Reg 90 Rounded, slightly cupped and fluted leaves having a deep zone RHSCC 200B deepening to 200A, and a centre yellow-green butterfly marking RHSCC 160A. Double many petalled flowers with some petaloids. Eight to ten florets form compact flower heads held well above the foliage on reddish stems. Flower colour clear scarlet-red RHSCC 44B. Compact, self-branching growth to 15 cm (6"). Long flowering period. A delightful miniature for container or rock garden.

'Occold Embers' Gold leaf with chestnut zone toward edge of leaf. Double flowers, glowing salmon, overlaid pink, RHSCC 41B/C. Self branching, compact dwarf plant. Bedding or container growing.

'Red Black Vesuvius' Small, almost black leaves with broad black zone. Single red flowers in abundance. Dwarf growing plant ideal for the rock garden, border or a container. **(Plate 49)**

'Retah's Brownie' Green leaves with dark centre blotch darkening in winter. Outside edge of leaf finely lined brownish red. Older leaves show distinct reddish sheen. Single salmon-red flowers in abundance. Strong growth. Good garden plant. Also useful as cut material, in winter, for floral arrangements.

'Robert Fish' Green-gold unzoned leaves, turning pure gold in Winter. Small, single vermilion flowers RHSCC 40A. Free flowering. Growth slender and lax growing to a height of 60 cm (2') if supported. Good for decorative work. A sport from 'Robert Fish' is 'Golden Butterfly' with the leaves showing a distinct butterfly type zone of yellow-gold in the centre. Flowers and growth habit similar to the parent.

'Silver Kewense' Small, green leaves edged white, occasionally tinged violet. Single, narrow petalled flowers, currant red. Small, miniature plant. Container growing.

'Spanky' Rg 29 Silver tri-colour. Green leaves unevenly splashed and zoned in centre with red RHSCC 39A/B. Outer edges yellow 11C. Colours distinct and uniform. New leaves and winter growth particularly well coloured. Growth upright and strong, needs pinching to make bushy. An improvement on 'Miss Burdett Coutts' being easier to grow and maintaining good colour. Excellent container plant. A similar plant is 'Lillian Lance' which is scarce. **(Plate 46)**

'Tunia's Delight' Gold leaves with irregular buff zone in winter. Single red flowers. Medium habit of growth. Good container plant.

'Variegated Kleiner Liebling' Very small, crinkled grey-green leaves bordered white. Small single rose-pink flowers, based white on upper petals. The green leaved plant from which the variegated form sported, is known as 'Kleiner Liebling', 'Little Darling' or 'Petit Pierre'. Excellent container plants or for small pockets in the rock garden.

Ivy-Leaved Pelargoniums

'Apricot Queen' Medium sized apricot-salmon flowers, the centres of which turn white as they age. Free flowering, strong, small wooded making a compact plant. Container, or ground cover plant.

'Blauer Frühling' ('Blue Spring') Double flowers of mallow-purple/bluish mauve. Soft green downy foliage, branching and upright, making a compact growing plant. Belonging to the group known as Hybrid-ivy leaved pelargoniums, ideal plants for window boxes, containers or the garden. **(Plate 71)**

'Bridesmaid' Double flowers soft orchid pink RHSCC 73D, upper petals blotched and feathered 57A. Free flowering on long stems. Strong growth, compact and ideal for container growing. **(Plate 70)**

'Butterflies' Single, medium to large flowers cyclamen purple RHSCC 84B (nearest). Thin stemmed, compact growing, large plant. Responds well to pinch pruning. Good for hanging basket, ground cover or spilling over walls and terraces.

'Carlos Uhden' Double bright, light red flowers opening to a white centre. Medium long stems making a compact plant. Good for hanging baskets, containers or spilling over walls.

'Dr Chipault' Double flowers, cerise-purple, with lighter reverse. Strong growing, compact plant flowering over a long period. Good for hanging baskets, spilling over walls.

'Duke of Edinburgh' Green leaves with cream variegation around the edges. Small single pink flowers in Spring and Summer. Strong growing plant which does well in baskets, or spilling over walls. The name is sometimes confused with 'Sunset' and 'Madame Margot'. **(Plate 63)**

'Galilee' Double bright pink—sometimes described as "Toothpaste pink". RHSCC 68B (nearest). Loose rosette type flowers. Medium growth habit and free flowering. Good container with support, or spilling over walls and hanging baskets. **(Plate 60)**

'Her Majesty the Queen' Double medium sized flowers, salmon-pink. Strong, medium sized plant. Constantly in bloom. Good basket plant or spilling over walls.

'Jester' ('The Jester') Double orchid-pink RHSCC 74C/D (nearest). Edges of petals finely pencilled or striped 57C (nearest). Exceptionally free blooming plant. Medium habit. Excellent container plant. 'El Gaucho' a sport of 'Jester' is equally good for container growing. **(Plate 62)**

'L' Elegante' Small dark green leaves margined white, the white changing to pink and mauve when grown hard and dry. Leaves are brittle and have a fruity scent. Flowers large, single, white with red-purple feathering. Free flowering. Dwarf compact growth. An ideal container plant. **(Plate 68)**

'La France' Semi-double to double loosely formed large flowers of deep lavender with darker feathering. Fast growing and free flowering. Good for spilling over walls, large containers or covering fences. Sometimes sports to a lighter coloured form known as 'Sport of La France' **(Plate 66 and 59)**. Other similar plants are 'Amethyst' and 'Dark Amethyst'.

'Leopard' Double orchid pink flowers RHSCC 68C, blotched rose-red to crimson. Medium growth. A good basket plant. 'Carnival', a similar plant, is a sport of 'Leopard'.

'Madame Crousse' Semi-double soft mauve-pink flowers RHSCC 68B (nearest). Thought to be the same as 'Comtesse de Grey'. A well known plant having been grown in Australia for many years. Good for trailing over walls, covering fences, large containers.

'Mexican Beauty' Semi-double blood red flowers. A sport from 'Comtesse de Grey' to which it will often revert. Long trailing plant, free flowering. A combination of 'Mrs. Banks' white, with 'Madame Crousse' and 'Mexican Beauty' makes a very colourful spill-over effect. Equally good for climbing (with support). **(Plate 67)**

'Millfield Gem' Double blush white to soft pink flowers, blotched rose-red on upper petals. Soft medium green foliage on a compact growing plant. Buds appear like tiny rose buds, opening more fully as they age. A sport of 'Millfield Gem' known as 'Millfield Rosebud' or 'Rosebud Gem' has flowers remaining as tiny rose-bud type blooms. These plants belong to the group known as Hybrid-ivy leaved pelargoniums, others of which are 'Lady Gertrude', 'Achievement', 'Schone Schwarzwaldern' ('Forest Maid') and 'Blauer Fruhling' ('Blue Spring'). Rust resistant plants requiring little pruning or shaping, they are good for garden, container or hanging basket.

'**Monty**' Large double orange-red. Vigorous growth yet compact. Long flowering season in good position with plenty of sun. Container or spill-over.

'**Mrs H.J. Jones**' ('**Pink Carnation**') Double flowers phlox pink RHSCC 68A (nearest). Edges of petals serrated and striped with a deeper colour giving the impression of a carnation. Unusual and beautiful. Medium growth, ideal for container growing, flowering abundantly.

'**Princess Victoria**' Large semi-double flowers, white flushed pale pink, with crimson stripes and faint pencilling on edge of petals. Leaves sometimes slightly cupped. Slow growing compact habit. A beautiful and interesting novelty ideal for hanging baskets or containers. May sometimes revert to 'Rose Enchantress' and such growth should be removed and grown as a separate plant. Not the original 'Princess Victoria' which was pale lilac.

'**Rouletta**' ('**Mexikanerin**') Semi-double blood red, striped white. Flowers produced in profusion and are quite outstanding. Long trailing habit of growth similar to the plant from which it sported i.e. 'Mexican Beauty'. Any growth showing flower colour reversions should be removed. Good for spilling over walls, large urns, climbing (with support) or can be trained as an espalier. (**Plate 64**)

'**Silver Jubilee**' Rg 76 Double, tight florets of dark purple RHSCC 77A, green at centre. White reverse to petals. Light green, small leaves. Short distances between the nodes on stems, growth compact. Ideal for hanging baskets and containers.

'**Sugar Baby**' ('**Pink Gay Baby**') Small double rose-pink flowers with deeper markings on upper petals. Flowers held on long stems above the foliage. Miniature leaves and dwarf prostrate growth. Profuse blooming. Good ground cover or container plant. A similar plant 'Gay Baby' with even smaller flowers of double white, lilac tinted, is also a miniature ivy-leaved pelargonium. Equally good for ground cover or container but slow growing and not so free flowering as the pink form. (**Plate 65**)

'**Sybil Holmes**' Double rose-pink, rosebud type flowers, slow to open. Compact dwarf growing plant almost always covered with flowers. A sport of 'Sybil Holmes' known as 'Sybil's Tu Tu' Rg 84, has rose-pink flowers with edges of petals pencilled deeper and very ruffled. Both good for ground cover or baskets.

'**The Duchess**' Large semi-double flowers, white faintly flushed orchid, with rose-purple pencilling on all petals. Upper petals feathered and blotched Tyrian Purple. Dark green leaves showing a small centre zone in winter. A small wooded plant which blooms well. 'Valencia' and 'Caprice' are both considered to be sports from 'The Duchess'. Good plants for container growing.

'**White Mesh**' ('**Sussex Lace**') Semi-double soft mauve-pink flowers the same as those of 'Madame Crousse'. Leaves coarsely meshed creamy white. Considered to be a sport of 'Madame Crousse'. Medium to long growth good for container growing or spilling over walls. Not to be confused with the plant called 'The Crocodile' ('Crocodile') which has similarly veined or meshed leaves but in a much finer pattern, and single vermilion flowers. ('White Mesh' **Plate 61**)

Regal Pelargoniums

'**Apollo**' Deep ox-blood-red flowers with black blotch on all petals. Flowers large, open and frilled. Growth dense and bushy. Garden or container. (**Plate 79**)

'**Applause**' Rose-pink flowers with a white throat, white edges to the petals. Five to seven petals per flower, all petals extremely ruffled. Free branching, bushy plant which flowers in abundance. Garden or container.

'**Baby Snooks**' Pale orchid pink flowers, top petals veined rose-violet with deep red blotches in the centre, flushed raspberry toward the petal edges. A miniature regal pelargonium. Flowers and foliage small in keeping with the miniature habit of the plant. Profuse bloomer, ideal for container growing or in the garden in front of a taller growing regal.

'**Blue Bird**' Rg 10 Blue-mauve flowers with silver sheen. Upper petals RHSCC 78C/B, blotched deep purple-black. Lower petals 84B, feathered 74B. Leaves soft green and rounded. Growth compact and sturdy. Good container or garden plant. (**Plate 83**)

'**Bodey's Picotee**' Very dark wine-red almost black, distinct pale pink/white edge to all petals. Flowers have rich velvety appearance. Strong growth. Good for garden or container.

'**Chorus Girl**' Unusual salmon flowers edged light lavender, with narrow lavender throat. Petals ruffled. Mass early bloomer improving as the season progresses, and continuing to flower over a long period. Garden or container. (**Plate 78**)

'**Cundare**' Rg 113 White flowers almost entirely blotched Cardinal red RHSCC 53B, veined 59A. Small flowers with pointed petals giving the effect of being more red than white. Leaves light green with slight perfume. Low growing, short noded plant, early flowering, in abundance. (**Plate 80**)

'**Dodie**' Rg 103 Flowers currant red RHSCC 47A veined and flushed 185A. Top petals small dark blotch 187A, light throat. Rounded flowers with waved edges. Light green maple shaped leaves with lightly serrated edges. Compact, self branching, medium sized plant. Flowering early Spring to Autumn. (**Plate 81**)

'**Fanta**' Rg 78 Large frilled flowers, azalea pink to orange RHSCC 41C. White throat, edge and reverse of petals. Upper petals blotched and feathered. Medium sized truss. Light green leaves. Compact medium growth. Flowering mid to late Summer.

'**Fire Glow**' Large flowers of glowing intense red, almost black blotches on upper petals. A most striking colour. Large heads on a well branched, strong plant. Garden or container. (**Plate 92**)

'**First Blush**' White upper petals, flushed soft crimson-rose RHSCC 50A/52A, small purple feathering. Lower petals white, unmarked. Medium sized flowers on a medium growing strong plant. Garden or container.

'**Flamenco**' Rg 19 Flowers rose madder/soft dusty pink with waved petals. Upper petals heavily blotched and feathered deep mulberry-red. Lower petals lighter in colour with faint feathering. Short jointed plant with grey-green foliage. Spring flowering, continued occasional flowers until Autumn. Garden or container. (**Plate 87**)

'**Funny Girl**' Rg 4 Deep rose flowers shading through salmon. Upper petals heavily blotched maroon, lower petals smaller blotches and feathering. All petals edged rose-pink, white throat. Flowers held on tall stems well above the foliage. Deep green leaves on a shrubby tall plant. Good garden specimen. (**Plate 77**)

'**Garnet Wings**' Rg 86 Peony purple flowers RHSCC 59A fading to a lighter centre 70A, white throat. All petals small dark blotch and feathering. Ruffled flowers. Soft green leaves with lightly serrated edges on a compact self-branching medium sized plant. Garden or container. (**Plate 72**)

'**Gemini**' Soft flesh pink shading to clear white throat. Upper petals sometimes veined and feathered crimson. Lower petals plain colour. Some flowers have more than five petals giving an effect of doubling. Soft green foliage on a short and bushy plant. Container or garden.

'Georgia Peach' Five to seven petalled flowers of pure clear peach-pink colour. Cup shaped flowers with waved edges. A most unusual and beautiful plant. Dark green leaves. Growth branching, inclined to be a little straggly, without shaping. The flower colour shows up well under artificial light when used for floral arrangements. Two Australian regals of similar pure colour and cup shaped flowers are 'Whisper' Rg 106 delicate pale mauve and 'Gentle Georgia' Rg 105 pastel pink. Good container plants with shaping, or garden.

'Golden Princess' Pure white flowers. Foliage variegated green and gold. Slow grower. An unusual novelty arising as a sport on 'Grace Armstrong', a white flowered form with slight markings of mauve on the upper petals and plain green leaves.

'Goldie' Rg 85 Golden salmon flowers with white base to all petals. Upper petals RHSCC 43B feathered 185A. Lower petals 43C. Large wavy petals. Deep green leaves, serrated edges. Strong growing, stocky plant. Flowering mid season, garden variety. (Plate 93)

'Grand Slam' Rose red with a slight salmon sheen. Upper petals blotched strawberry-black with slight veining. Touch of white near throat. Compact, free flowering, self branching plant excellent for garden or container growing. (Plate 91)

'Happy Valley' Large flowers of ruffled pink, veined raspberry. Burgundy-maroon marks on upper petals. Large truss. Growth strong and good. Garden or large container plant. A sport from this plant has been introduced as 'Monreith'.

'Harvest Moon' Flowers of several shades of salmon-apricot, and having beautifully ruffled petals. A naturally well shaped, strong growing plant good for garden or container. There is also a zonal pelargonium by this name. (Plate 90)

'Isadora' Rg 13 Deep orchid-pink RHSCC 68B/A, white throat with red feathering. Upper petals flushed 52B. Large well formed heads with extremely ruffled flowers giving the effect of doubling. Small, rounded grey-green leaves. Short, bushy growth. Container or garden. (Plate 86)

'Joan Morf' White flowers shaded soft rose-pink RHSCC 65A/B. Upper petals feathered 67A. Delicately ruffled blooms on a compact self branching plant. Garden or container. (Plate 73)

'Josephine' Light rosy pink with white throat. An old variety, sparse growing plant which needs shaping, but a favourite for continued flowering throughout the year. Excellent garden plant. There is also a zonal pelargonium named 'Josephine'.

'Larabelle' Rg 66 Double soft rose pink RHSCC 65A with markings of 53B showing well down in the centre of each flower. The number of petals varies from thirteen to seventeen. Flower buds form on long stalks and are held well clear of the foliage. The flower when open gives the impression of a camellia. A distinct and interesting plant. Strong thick stemmed growth of loose habit. Shaping is necessary to produce a good plant. Garden or container (if shaped). Another double flowering regal is 'Phyllis Richardson' a much softer pink. Also strong growing plant which needs shaping. 'Larabelle' (Plate 85)

'Little Love' ('Love and Kisses') Small orchid mauve with a creamy white base. A sport of the well-known 'All My Love' in miniature form. A good container plant or equally good for the garden.

'Madame Layal' ('Mme. Layal') Five petalled, rounded flower, referred to as a "Pansy" pelargonium. Upper petals purple, lower mainly white. Small flowers on a small growing miniature type,

regal pelargonium plant. Growth compact. Good container plant or garden specimen.

'Maja' Carmine-rose. Top petals RHSCC 57D heavily blotched 59A. Lower petals 61D feathered 44A. Rounded flowers on a compact, strong growing plant. Garden or container. (Plate 88)

'Mariquita' Medium strawberry pink flowers with bright strawberry pink markings on upper petals, small deeper markings on lower petals. Extremely large flowers up to 10 cm (4″) across. Strong upright growth. Good garden plant or large container.

'Miss Australia' Deep azalea pink flowers RHSCC 40B feathered 46A, small white throat. Leaves mid-green, slightly cupped, edged with white. Habit of growth tall and straggly like its parent 'Azalea' ('Azaleaflora') from which it sported. 'Miss Perth' and 'Snow Festival' are two other variegated foliaged regal pelargoniums. 'Snow Festival' (Plate 37)

'Monreith' Rg 107 Flowers white, flushed deep pink RHSCC 55B, barred RHSCC 53C. Upper petals veined dark cardinal red RHSCC 53A. Unusual shaped flowers with upper petals pointed. Leaves medium green. Growth compact, height medium. Flowering Spring through Summer. A distinctive and unusual novelty. Excellent container plant.

'Ostergruss' ('Easter Greeting') Flowers cerise rose RHSCC 67C with each petal blotched 187A. An old cultivar raised in Germany in 1899. Still grown for its early and repeat flowering. A branched, low growing plant, inclined to be straggly, it has the occasional flowers throughout the year as well as the usual Spring flush. Garden or container.

'Picador' Rg 15 Wine red, small blotches of chestnut colour on upper petals. Large flowers with a silvery sheen. Soft green rounded leaves on a low growing, bushy plant. Container or garden.

'Rembrandt' Rg 16 Deep pansy purple, edged pale lavender. Upper petals deep purple, lower petals slightly lighter, lavender throat shading to white. Large flowers with waved petals, and showing the prominent orange stamens. A striking and popular plant for garden or container. (Plate 74)

'Snow Festival' Rg 73 Flowers large, phlox purple RHSCC 75B. Upper petals almost completely covered with black blotch, flushed 71B, edged 75B. Lower petals 75B unmarked. Leaves grey-green 191B, edged white. Quite distinct. Upright growth, with short noded stems. Spring and Summer flowering. (Plate 37)

'Strawberry Sundae' Bright strawberry pink with white throat. Upper petals RHSCC 52A, heavily blotched and veined 187A. Lower petals light strawberry pink, white flushed, veined 55A/B. Medium growing plant blooming early and continuing over a long period. Good container plant. (Plate 75)

'Tarantella' Pale orchid-pink RHSCC 69A. Top petals almost entirely blotched magenta purple 61A. Lower petals lightly veined 70B. Extremely ruffled flowers with the stamens prominently displayed. Compact growth. Container or garden plant. (Plate 82)

'Tarli' Rg 102 Large florets, waved petals of jasper red, RHSCC 39A, top petals blotched deep purple/brown RHSCC 187A. Large white centre to florets, and white petal edges. Leaves soft green. Medium growth. Good container plant with a long flowering season from early Spring to late Summer.

'Tunia's Perfecta' Flowers of orange colouring with brown overcast. RHSCC 46B. Upper petals blotched and veined 187B.

White throat. Large showy blooms, slightly ruffled. Low growing bushy plant. Container or garden.

'Virginia'   Pure white. Large well shaped blooms with lightly ruffled petals. Long flowering season. Garden or container. Other whites include 'White Champion' and 'Aquarius' Rg 9. (**Plate 84**)

'Waltztime'   Large flowers with six to seven petals slightly ruffled. Soft lavender RHSCC 75B (nearest). Upper petals slightly darker, veined and blotched crimson/purple. Excellent plant for use in floral work. Early flowering. A garden or container plant. Sometimes sports to a pink form known as 'Pink Waltz Time'.

'Wine Festival' Rg 17   Light wine red flowers RHSCC 58B/C. Each petal heavily blotched deep burgundy, almost black. Six to seven petals per flower. Light green leaves, serrated edges. Strong growth and long flowering season. Garden or container. (**Plate 89**)

Species Derived Pelargoniums including Scented-Leaved Species

'Catford Belle'   Small single flowers of rose-purple RHSCC 68A. Upper petals marked cyclamen purple. Thin, rather woody stems, bushy growth. Small green leaves, zoneless. One of a group known as the "Angel Pelargoniums" having a similarity in leaf and plant growth to the *Pelargonium crispum* species. Others include 'Rose Bengal', 'Kerlander' and 'Mrs. Dumbrill'.

'Clorinda'   Single bright rose-pink flowers, RHSCC 67C, upper petals flushed and feathered 57C/B. Flowers and three lobed leaves, large for this group. Leaves faintly scented. Compact, branching, erect growth. Container or garden.

'Lady Plymouth'   Small single pale mauve flowers. Leaves grey-green, edged cream, rose scented. Compact branching habit. May grow to one metre in height under good conditions. Foliage excellent for floral work. Container plant or open garden.

'Lara Starshine' Rg 41   Single carmine-rose flowers, upper petals tinged on top half RHSCC 64C. Lower petals 52C with slight veining. A *Pelargonium radens* (Syn. *P. radula*) hybrid with improved flower size and colour. Leaf shape, colour and perfume similar to *P. radens*. Naturally branching, compact growth. Spring, Summer and Autumn flowering. Height 60 cm (2′) when grown in container. Larger growth in the open garden (**Plate 76**, also on front of cover)

'Madame Nonin' ('Mme. Nonin')   Small flowers neyron-rose RHSCC 55A. Petals broad and curled giving an impression of doubling. Dark green leaves on a branching, medium growing plant. Good garden plant, older leaves turning Autumn colourings in colder weather.

'Mabel Grey'   Heavily perfumed citron. Single purple flowers on a tall growing, sparse plant. Leaves dark green, rough textured with serrated edges. Considered the most strongly perfumed of all the scented-leaved pelargoniums.

Pelargonium crispum   Strong lemon scent. Small pale lavender flowers appearing individually down the stem. Leaves small, curled and fluted, with long stalks. Shrubby, branched upright growth on slender woody stems. Height to approximately 90 cm (3′) in good position. Interesting forms of *P. crispum* are *P. crispum* 'Minor' ("Fingerbowl Pelargonium") and *P. crispum* 'Variegated' ('Variegated Crispum'), ('Variegated Prince Rupert'). The *P. crispum* 'Variegated' is sometimes called 'French Lace' and has leaves edged white. Valuable for floral work and container growing. (**Plate 24**)

Pelargonium fragrans   (Nutmeg scented)   Strong scent of spice or nutmeg. Small, slightly lobed, round crinkled grey-green leaves. Tiny white flowers, red veins on upper petals in clusters on a branched, leafy, rangy plant. Growth to approximately 60 cm (2′). There is also a variegated form known as 'Variegated Fragrans' or 'Variegated Nutmeg'. Both good container or garden plants.

Pelargonium X *nervosum* (Lime scented)   Strong scent of lime. Leaves small, deep green, smooth and toothed. Single small lavender flowers with dark markings. Compact erect growth. Good container plant or garden specimen.

Pelargonium odoratissimum (Apple scented)   Strong apple scent. Light green leaves, oval shaped, ruffled and velvety to the touch. Tiny white flowers with upper petals having small red pin points. Thin stemmed, almost vine-like branches bear the tiny flowers. Compact shrubby growth. Good rockery plant, border for garden path or container. (**Plate 23**)

Pelargonium tomentosum (Peppermint scented)   Strong peppermint scent. Large grey-green leaves with soft velvety touch, hairy and shaped like a grape leaf. Tiny white flowers with some purple veining. A handsome spreading, bushy, plant growing to a height of about 60 cm (2′) and a spread of at least one metre if left unchecked. Well suited for planting beside a pathway. Other *P. tomentosum* type plants are 'Dark Lady' and 'Joy Lucille' both having a decided peppermint scent.

'Rollison's Unique' ('Rollisson's Unique')   Single tyrian purple flowers RHSCC 61C, veined and feathered 57A. Upper petals slightly larger. Leaves soft and downy, large and slightly crinkled, with a slight scent. Medium growth, erect, sometimes sending out long rangy stems which will climb if given support. Good for garden where it can be left to ramble.

'Scarlet Pet'   Small Turkey-red flowers, upper petals veined darker, almost black. Dark green leaves partly divided. Habit of growth straggly, erect semi-dwarf. Moderate flowering throughout the year. An old favourite. Garden, or large container if shaped.

'White Unique'   Medium sized white flowers tinted pale rose-purple RHSCC 68D, upper petals feathered 68A. Three lobed, triangular shaped leaves, faintly scented. Large busy, branching plant with woody stems. Height to about 60 cm (2′). Good garden plant or container.

Unusual Species for the Collector

Pelargonium acetosum   Small, bushy plant with slender branches. Leaves smooth, shiny and scalloped, with a thin reddish margin. Flowers single salmon-pink. Two upper petals thin, erect, held closely together and with distinct veining. Lower petals thin, broadly spaced apart and a much paler rose-pink. Stamens clearly visible. Flowering may be at any time of the year. Grows well on stony sloping ground. Some work has been done with this plant and selected zonal cultivars. Two such hybrids being 'Irma' and 'Frills'.

Pelargonium betulinum (Birch-leaf *pelargonium*)   A shrubby, erect, but sometimes sprawling shrub, growing to about 60 cm (2′) and worthy of a place in the garden. Leaves are small, almost hairless and toothed on the margins which sometimes become red tinged. The single flowers are lavender pink to purple, sometimes with darker streaks. The upper petals broader and darker than the lower. When in full flower the plant is quite conspicuous, flowers being produced from early Spring through Summer. Does well in coastal areas in sandy soil.

Pelargonium carnosum (*Carnosus*—fleshy or succulent)   An interesting species with thick succulent stems, swollen at the joints and much branched. Leaves much divided and smooth, although much variability in leaf form may be seen in the wild.

Flowers are single, small, varying from white to greenish-yellow with reddish streaks on the two slightly larger upper petals. Flowers produced from January to March. Height about 60 cm (2'). Does well in dry and slightly clayey areas.

Pelargonium ceratophyllum A rather straggly plant with succulent stems, swollen at the nodes. Leaves fleshy and finely divided. Flowers single, white with upper two slightly broader and spotted red at the base. Height to 60 cm (2'). This species is mostly listed under *P. crithmifolium* of which it may be a variant.

Pelargonium cordifolium (Syn. *P. cordatum*) Tall growing plant with cordate shaped leaves shallowly lobed. Leaves usually lighter in colour on the under-side and with a soft hairy texture. Single pink-purple flowers, two upper petals veined and feathered dark purple. Lower petals thin and narrow, much lighter in colour and with the stamens clearly visible. Growth tall, branched and spreading to a height of approximately 1 metre. Prefers a slightly more moist area than many of the species.

Pelargonium cotyledonis (**"Old Man Live for Ever"**) This rare species comes from the Island of St. Helena. Dwarf growing, spreading plant with thick succulent stems. Broadly ovate leaves, almost undivided, hairy underneath when young. The plant is deciduous, at this time needing little or no water. Single small, rounded, five petalled, pure white flowers, held on tall thin stems well above the foliage. A connoisseur's delight.

Pelargonium echinatum (**"Sweetheart Geranium"**) An unusual species having succulent stems with spine-like stipules, tuberous roots and deciduous leaves. Flowers are borne on thin stems. Single white, with crimson-purple blotches on upper petals which are slightly larger than the lower. Sometimes the lower petals are also spotted. Leaves kidney to heart shaped, very slightly lobed, and of a grey-green colour. The underside of the leaf is lighter in colour and more hairy. The colour of the flower varies with age showing two colours on the one head. There is a purple-magenta flowered form known as 'Miss Stapleton' or *Pelargonium echinatum stapletonii*. Good container plant. Needs to be kept dry when not in leaf. Flowering is Winter and early Spring.

Pelargonium gibbosum (**"Gouty Geranium"**) A night perfumed plant of unusual growth habit and flower colour. Greenish-yellow flowers, single, highly perfumed at dusk. Leaves grey-green, fleshy, and unusually divided, with two lateral leaflets separated by about 2 cm (1") from the upper section which is three lobed. Stems are strangely knotted or swollen at the nodes. Growth spreading and will even climb with support. Open garden or rock garden plant where it can be left to spread naturally. ·

Pelargonium hirtum (*Hirtum*—hairy) A bushy shrubby plant attaining a height of about 30 cm (12"). Slender branches which are of a greyish colour and rather thick and fleshy. The finely divided leaves are rather like those of a carrot, but are usually covered with long and soft hairs—hence the name—*hirtum*. Flowers are single, small, bright pink to purple with darker spots at the base of the two upper petals. The two upper petals are slightly larger than the lower. Usually flowers from mid Winter through to mid Summer. Grows well in sandy soil or on rocky ledges.

Pelargonium rodneyanum An Australian species with small to medium deep pink-purple flowers. Stems very short, if any, and dark green, slightly five to seven lobed leaves. A perennial plant making an effective clump with many flowers held above the foliage on medium to tall stems. Grows well in rocky granite type country. A paler pink form has been found.

Pelargonium sulphureum A small stemless plant with tuberous root and simple leaves. Flowers are held on tall stems above the foliage and are of a pale primrose colour with dark spots and sometimes dark veins or lines. Height about 15.2 cm (6") to 30 cm (12"). Does well in sandy or dry clayey positions. Mostly listed under *Pelargonium longifolium* at the present time.

Pelargonium tetragonum (**"Square stemmed pelargonium"**) Succulent plant requiring dry conditions. Bushy habit, branching from the base and sprawling among and up other plants sometimes reaching a height of about 60 cm (2'). Thin, brittle stems, four sided with distinct joints, or nodes. Dull green leaves, with a darker central mark, occur at these joints, and are small and fleshy. The four petalled flowers are very prominent, the two upper petals being much larger than the lower pair. Usually creamy-white in colour to pale pink, with deep red stripes on the upper petals. The stamens are clearly seen. An interesting plant for a dry rocky situation. (**Plate 25**)

Pelargonium triste (**"Sad Geranium"**—**"Night scented Geranium"**) Reputedly the first *Pelargonium* to be transported from the Cape of Good Hope in the 17th century. A tuberous rooted plant with leaves like those of a carrot. Flowers are small, dull coloured yellowish-green to brownish-purple with a lighter, almost yellow margin. Flower colours vary slightly. Strongly night scented with a musk-like perfume. Leaves die off during the plant's dormant period when little or no water is required. Does well in sandy or gravelly soils.

Pelargonium violarium (*P. violaceae.*—*P. tricolor arborea*) A half shrubby perennial growing to about 30 cm (12"). The main stem is short with many side branches, making a low compact plant. Long narrow grey-green leaves slightly hairy. Single flowers, upper petals white base almost covered with dark red-purple, and having a shiny dark spot at the base. Lower petals white, sometimes with a narrow red streak from the base. Does well in a sandy position in the garden or makes a good container specimen. (**Plate 21**)

10. FLOWER PRODUCTION

One of the major objects in growing pelargoniums is to enjoy the flower, whose shape and colour excites our aesthetic senses. In this chapter some of the factors affecting the flowering of the plant are examined. We begin by defining some basic terms.

Firstly, what is a flower? A flower is a group of closely crowded specialized leaves at the end of a short branch including one or more of the following kinds of members: sepals, petals, stamens and carpels. The latter includes the ovary, style and stigma. Readers are referred to the diagram given in Appendix 1 which shows a flower and its component parts. The basic petal arrangement of a pelargonium is five petals but in some flowers the stamens may grow into petals producing the so-called double flowers.

In the zonal and ivy-leaved pelargoniums the *inflorescence* (or bundle of flowers) is readily seen as such, consisting of a few to many flowers, each flower being on a green stalk all of equal length and all seeming to arise from a single point on the stem of the inflorescence. The diagram of Appendix 1 shows this clearly, an examination of a live flower will show it even better. This form of inflorescence is called an *umbel*. In the regal pelargonium a few flowers, usually three or four, form an umbel but there are usually several such umbels on a common flower stalk (the *peduncle*) so the inflorescence in this case becomes a compound umbel. It is usual for pelargoniums to have several inflorescences existing at the same time.

Factors affecting flower initiation

As early as the 1850's horticulturists believed that the length of daylight periods had an influence on flowering. In 1879 Edison invented the incandescent lamp which allowed the daylight period to be extended and it was demonstrated that the flowering of some plants could be made to occur earlier than usual. Conversely for some other species the flowering was inhibited entirely, in others it appeared to make little difference.

This subsequently led, in the 1920's to the concept of short and long day plants. The *Pelargonium* was regarded as a day neutral plant, the length of the daylight period being of no importance. This line of thought inhibited further experimental work on this genus as there seemed little profit in working with a plant which did not respond. It was not until the 1960's and 1970's that further work was spurred on by the extensive potted plant sales of pelargoniums in the USA.

Pelargoniums are basically spring flowering plants, buds being initiated in the colder months of the year. If the weather, after the spring flush of flowers continues to be cold, further bud initiation will occur if the newer growth has not been pruned. This further flush is also promoted by the increasing length of daylight period and light intensity at this time of the year.

Experimental work has shown that low temperature promotes the production of flowers whereas high temperatures suppresses flowering. This suppression may be reduced by exposing the plants to a longer period of light using electric lamps.

For Spring flowering a night temperature of 13°C or lower is desirable for July/August (southern hemisphere). If this temperature is not attained, as may happen in the more northern climates, then the warmer temperatures may be offset by exposing the plants to sixteen hours of light. This can be made up of daylight for as long as possible, say nine hours of daylight followed by seven hours of electric light from incandescent bulbs. The latter give more red light than fluorescent lamps and red light is significant in flower promotion. As incandescent lamps produce a lot of heat the bulb should not come closer than about 70 cms from the top of the plant. A 100 watt bulb will then produce about 40 foot-candles of light intensity at the top of the plant. Usually several plants may be irradiated from a single bulb. Forced air flow for cooling may also be desirable unless the room is well ventilated.

As well as being used to offset the higher winter temperatures this method may be used to hasten flowering to meet a target date, a flower show, a birthday gift and so on.

Although plants grow in open spaces in full sunshine this does not necessarily mean that such conditions are optimum. As far as flowering is concerned about one-third the intensity of full summer sunshine seems sufficient. In areas where winter temperature is sufficiently low and the days are sunny the plants, may be brought into a protected area away from insects when the buds are about to form.

Pruning and shaping the plant is not only advisable for aesthetic reasons but it also multiplies the number of flowers produced by the plant. Many *Pelargonium* cultivars, if allowed to grow naturally will produce long and unbranched stems with a single inflorescence at the top. New growth and side branching will produce flowers, so adequate pruning and pinching is needed. This aspect of culture is covered in the chapter *Pruning & Shaping*.

Although flower initiation is caused by growth substances (often called hormones) produced within the plant the actual production of flowers needs food and energy in much the same way as leaf development depends on food supply and energy. There is little doubt that a well grown plant, hence a well fertilized plant, will produce an abundance of flowers. Plants growing in a poor soil will ultimately flower but do so to the detriment of the plant which must transfer the necessary food and energy from its own meagre sources.

During the period leading up to flower development the plant should be given plenty of nutrients. Water soluble fertilizers are a convenient method of adding to the nutrients already in the potting mix. There is no one nutrient which promotes flower initiation and growth, notwith-standing such attributes sometimes applied to any one of these. It has often been reported that nitrogen may be omitted from a fertilizer when flowering is anticipated, presumably on the basis that no leaf growth, hence no protein is needed. This is fallacious. There is still normal tissue development necessary for the peduncle, pedicels, sepals and ovary and the flower cells contain cytoplasm. All of these require nitrogen for development and if this is not supplied the plant tissue will be robbed of this element. This may prevent other side shoots from producing a good show of flowers.

In temperate climates pelargoniums produce flowers abundantly if certain simple cultural procedures are adopted. The actual month of flowering will vary from north to south, from the mountains to the sea and to the dry hinterland but flower they will, which is one of the reasons for their popularity.

The production of flowering plants at a given date is not so simple. Some commercial growers use various growth retardants and other chemicals on their plants to produce flowers for a specified market. These substances are not readily available to the home grower and are not mentioned here. It has been advocated that some cultivars may be shocked into flowering by alternate drying out and wetting of the soil. This action is preceded by withholding fertilizer from the plant. If the drying out is done too enthusiastically the root system could well be damaged and although the plant may flower its future could be in jeopardy.

1. Seeds: *Pelargonium* (page 9)

2. *Pelargonium australe* (page 6)

3. Seeds: *Erodium* (page 9)

4. Arrangement using fancy-leaved foliage (page 37)

5. Seeds: *Geranium* (page 9)

6. *Erodium reichardii roseum* (page 35)

7. *Geranium pratense* (page 36)

49

8. *Geranium renardii* (page 36)

9. *Erodium supracanum* (page 35)

10. *Geranium dalmaticum* (page 36)

11. *Erodium manescavi* (page 35)

12. *Geranium pylzowianum* (page 35)

13. *Erodium hymenodes* (page 35)

14. Zonal pelargonium 'Multicolour' (page 39)

15. Zonal pelargonium 'Phlox Eye' (page 40)

16. Zonal pelargonium 'Apple Blossom Rosebud' (page 38)

17. Zonal pelargonium 'Red Demon' (page 40)

18. Zonal pelargonium 'Pink Poinsettia' (page 40)

19. Dwarf zonal pelargonium 'Orion' (page 40)

20. Zonal pelargonium 'Skelly's Pride' (page 40)

21. *Pelargonium violarium (P.violaceae)* (page 46)

22. *Erodium corsicum* var. *album* in the rock garden (page 35)

23. *Pelargonium odoratissimum* ("Apple Scented") (page 45)

24. *Pelargonium crispum* Variegated (page 45)

25. *Pelargonium tetragonum* (page 46)

26. Geraniums and Erodiums in the rock garden (page 35)

7. Unusual feature display for "geranium" (page 37)

28. Ivy-leaved pelargoniums used as spillovers (page 37)

29. Ivy-leaved pelargoniums as ground cover (page 37)

30. 'Madame Salleron' used as a border plant (page 36)

31. Flowering pelargoniums used as an effective border (page 37)

32. Decorative use for a hollowed-out log (page 37)

53

33. Zonal pelargonium 'Inspiration' (page 39)

34. Zonal pelargonium 'Xenia Field' (page 40)

35. Fancy-leaved zonal pelargonium 'Freak of Nature' (page 41)

36. Regal pelargonium grown as a "Standard" (page 37)

37. Fancy-leaved regal pelargonium 'Sn Festival' Reg 73 (page 44)

38. Zonal pelargonium 'Deacon Romance' (page 39)

39. Zonal pelargonium 'Magnificent' (page 39)

54

40. Fancy-leaved dwarf zonal pelargoniums 'Black Opal' 1 & 3 (page 36 & 40)

41. Dwarf zonal pelargonium 'Grannie Hewitt' ('Pigmy') (page 39)

42. Zonal pelargonium 'Wedding Day' Rg 18 (page 40)

43. Zonal pelargonium 'Encore' (page 39)

44. Zonal pelargonium 'Lavender Ricard' (page 39)

45. Zonal pelargonium 'Mrs Tarrant' (page 39)

46. Fancy-leaved zonal pelargonium 'Spanky' Rg 29 (page 42)

47. Fancy-leaved zonal pelargonium 'Mrs Strang' (page 41)

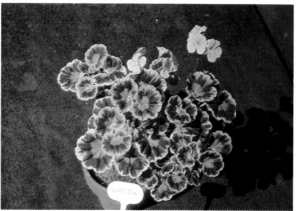

48. Fancy-leaved zonal pelargonium 'Mr Henry Cox' (page 41)

49. Dwarf fancy-leaved zonal pelargonium 'Red Black Vesuvius' (page 42)

50. Fancy-leaved zonal pelargonium 'Medallion' (page 41)

51. Fancy-leaved zonal pelargoniums 'Chelsea Gem' and 'Mrs Parker' (page 40)

2. Miniature fancy-leaved zonal pelargoniums 'Fairyland', 'Elf', 'Sprite' and 'Blazonry' (page 41)

53. Fancy-leaved zonal pelargonium 'Lass O'Gowrie' (page 41)

ancy-leaved zonal pelargonium 'Dolly arden' (page 41)

55. Fancy-leaved and flowering zonal pelargoniums used for bedding (page 36)

56. An arrangement using fancy-leaved foliage (page 37)

7. Fancy-leaved zonal pelargonium 'Masterpiece' (page 41)

58. Fancy-leaved zonal pelargonium 'Crystal Palace Gem' (page 40)

59. Ivy-leaved pelargonium 'Sport of La France' (page 42)

60. Ivy-leaved pelargonium 'Galilee' (page 42)

61. Fancy-leaved ivy pelargonium 'White Mesh' (page 43)

62. Ivy-leaved pelargonium 'Jester' (page 42)

63. Fancy-leaved ivy pelargonium 'Duke Edinburgh' ('Madame Margot') (page

64. Ivy-leaved pelargonium 'Rouletta' ('Mexikanerin') (page 43)

65. Ivy-leaved pelargonium 'Sugar Baby' ('Pink Gay Baby') (page

58

6. Ivy-leaved pelargonium 'La France' (page 42)

67. Ivy-leaved pelargonium 'Mexican Beauty' showing reversion (page 42)

8. Fancy-leaved ivy pelargonium 'L'Elegante' (page 42)

69. Ivy-leaved pelargoniums as ground cover (page 37)

70. Ivy-leaved pelargonium 'Bridesmaid' (page 42)

71. Hybrid-ivy leaved pelargonium 'Blauer Frühling' ('Blue Spring') (page 42)

72. Regal pelargonium 'Garnet Wings' Rg 86 (page 43)   73. Regal pelargonium 'Joan Morf' (page 44)

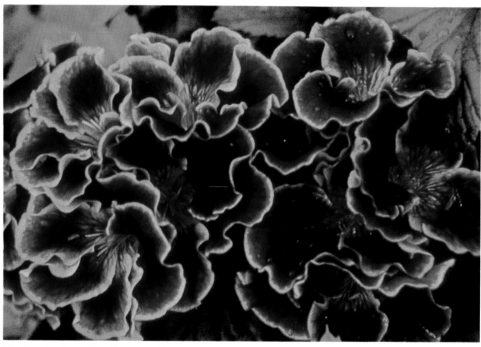

74. Regal pelargonium 'Rembrandt' Rg 16 (page 44)

75. Regal pelargonium 'Strawberry Sundae' (page 44)   76. Species derived pelargonium 'Lara Starshine' Rg 41 (page 45 and front cover)

77. Regal pelargonium 'Funny Girl' Rg 4 (page 43)

78. Regal pelargonium 'Chorus Girl' (page 43)

79. Regal pelargonium 'Apollo' (page 43)

80. Regal pelargonium 'Cundare' Rg 113 (page 43)

81. Regal pelargonium 'Dodie' Rg 103 (page 43)

82. Regal pelargonium 'Tarantella' (page 44)

83. Regal pelargonium 'Blue Bird' Rg 10 (page 43)

84. Regal pelargonium 'Virginia' (page 45)

85. Regal pelargonium 'Larabelle' Rg 66 (page 44)

86. Regal pelargonium 'Isadora' Rg 13 (page 44)

87. Regal pelargonium 'Flamenco' Rg 19 (page 43)

88. Regal pelargonium 'Maja' (page 44)

89. Regal pelargonium 'Wine Festival' Rg 17 (page 45)

90. Regal pelargonium 'Harvest Moon' (page 44)

91. Regal pelargonium 'Grand Slam' (page 44)

92. Regal pelargonium 'Fireglow' (page 43)

93. Regal pelargonium 'Goldie' Rg 85 (page 44)

94. Leaf showing symptoms of virus caused chlorosis (page 75)

95. Decorative arrangement using driftwood (page 37)

96. Decorative basket of zonal pelargonium flowers (page 37)

97. Leaf showing symptoms of bacterial leaf spot (page 75)

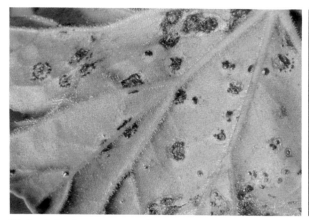

98. Leaf showing symptoms of rust pustules (page 74)

99. Decorative arrangement using 'Apple Blossom Rosebud' (page 3

11. CUT FLOWER PRESERVATION

Although the *Pelargonium* may be very effectively used as a pot plant for decoration many people prefer to use the cut flowers in floral art work or just as a table decoration for the home. The work entailed in making a floral arrangement is not inconsiderable so any tendency for the flowers to have a short life and premature petal fall is not conducive to their use. This chapter reviews some of the factors which produce premature failure of the flowers and suggests methods and solutions to overcome the problem.

If any of the flowers of the inflorescence have been open for a while and have been pollinated by insects the petals will fall and the inflorescence will be of little use in making any type of arrangement intended to last for a reasonable time. To avoid this problem potted flowering plants can be moved into an area protected from insects while garden plants can be protected by 'bagging' the inflorescence. Any open weave material such as a stocking is suitable for this.

As translocation of food within the plant is usually maximised at night, flowers cut in the early morning have some advantage over cutting later in the day. Placing the cut material into a bucket of water immediately after cutting is often advocated but this does not have any advantage if the floral material cannot be transferred directly from bucket to vase.

When cutting use a sharp knife for the final trim even if secateurs are used for the major cut as any use of blunt instruments will damage the very small water conducting channels in the stem. Diagonal cuts are satisfactory and for long stems or low containers such cutting keeps the water conducting vessels away from the base of the container.

There are four major factors which affect flower life. These are hygiene, temperature, water uptake, and food supply.

Hygiene

The cleanliness of the vase and vase water is important. Algal, fungal and bacterial growth in the vase solution can physically plug the water absorption tubes in the stem of the inflorescence.

Muddy water may also cause plugging so the provision of clear, clean water both physically and biologically is important in prolonging flower life in the vase.

The vase or container should be washed out thoroughly after and before use, using at least a household detergent. The compounds used for ensuring germ-free swimming pools are also useful disinfectants for this purpose. Avoid the phenolic disinfectants used for human wounds as failure to remove these may shorten flower life.

If cut leafy material is to be used to decorate the floral arrangement ensure that no leaves are left on the part of the stem which will be submerged in the water. This prevents contamination of the vase water by rotting leaves.

Temperature

The cut inflorescence should be kept at a low temperature until it is required, say at a minimum of five or six degrees Celsius when the atmosphere is also moist. Failing this the coolest spot available is recommended. A fan evaporating water from a wet canvas provides an ideal method of cooling as it also increases humidity and air circulation. Once the inflorescence has been cut from the plant it can no longer be supplied with food which it needs for its continued existence, therefore, it must rely on food stored in its own tissue. The object of cooling is to slow down the respiration rate of this tissue so decreasing both water and food usage. The floral arrangement or posy, once made, should be kept as cool as consistent with its intended use and so prolong life as long as possible.

Water uptake

The need for clean water has already been emphasized under the heading of Hygiene. There is, however, one other factor of equal importance. Acidic water is taken up more readily than neutral (e.g. city tap water) or alkaline water (bore water). To make vase water acidic add a small amount of citric acid which is both readily available and cheap, much cheaper than other substances often advocated. The preferred acidity of vase water should be a pH value of 3.5 to 4, that is more acid than say the water from a major city supply which is near neutral having a pH value of about 7. This acidity may be attained by adding 200 milligrams of citric acid to a litre of near neutral water, e.g. tap water. If the water is known to be alkaline, such as water from a bore, then additional citric acid should be used, say 300 milligrams per litre. Citric acid is a docile acid and a little excess will not do any harm, additionally it is a normal acid in plants so is not toxic to them. (200 milligrams of citric acid is just enough to cover a one cent piece when not heaped.)

Food supply

In many cases inflorescences are cut and placed in a container before all flower buds are open. If the buds are to grow and open both food and energy are needed. These are normally supplied by the green part of the plant from which the flowers have now been removed. The most abundant sugar circulating in plants is Sucrose, readily available in pure form as white table sugar. A 1.5% solution of this, fifteen grams (about ½ ounce) per litre of water will supply the plant with a natural food substance.

However such a solution is conducive to fungal growth so a fungicide needs to be added. Practically any fungicide will do but Captan has been used successfully. Sufficient of this dissolves in the water to inhibit fungal growth.

A recipe for vase water

To a litre of clean water of about neutral pH add 200 milligrams of citric acid, 15 grams of white sugar and 0.7 grams (about ¼ level teaspoon) of Captan, or equivalent other fungicide. Stir well to dissolve and mix. Some of the fungicide will remain in the bottom of the vessel. Pour desired amount into a clean vase.

In an experiment using this recipe compared with water, the flowers in the latter lasted for four days and the petals dropped, the buds remained static and did not open at all. The flowers in the recipe lasted much longer and most buds opened during the thirteen day experimental period. An inflorescence of regal pelargonium was still perfect at the end of the thirteen day period. Various inflorescences of zonal pelargoniums commenced to shrivel

after nine days but no petal fall occurred during the thirteen day period.

Other preserving substances

Experiments were conducted using other substances reported to be efficacious and the results are given below. All results are compared with tap water.

Chrysal This is an imported commercial product from Holland, marketed to assist in the preservation of cut flowers. On day six some of the older petals dropped but new buds were opening. On day nine some flowers were dying but new buds still opening although not of expected size. In tap water petal drop occurred during day seven.

Aspirin and *Aspro* Aspirin is the common name for acetyl salicylic acid and although this is an organic acid it does not occur naturally in plants. A 600 milligram tablet of aspirin was dissolved in 100 ml of water and reduced the pH to 4.4. *Aspro* is a trade name and one tablet of soluble *Aspro* contains aspirin, citric acid and sodium bicarbonate. When one tablet of this was dissolved in water the pH dropped to 5.6, the lower-acid reading being due to the antagonistic affect of the sodium bicarbonate which is alkaline in water solution.

Sugar (1.5%) was added to both solutions and cut material placed in each. Although the experiment was limited the result was not impressive and it would be hard to recommend this as opposed to the recipe given above.

Formula 20 This was used at the rate of two drops per litre. Some petal drop occurred in day five and continued throughout the experiment, bud opening was limited. This cannot be recommended as an additive in the concentration used.

Other factors

Ethylene gas in the minutest quantities can cause rapid death of flowers. This gas is given off by ripening fruit such as apples, bananas and pears, so keep the fruit bowl well away from your flower arrangements. There are substances which counter ethylene but the suitability of these for pelargoniums has not yet been shown so is outside the scope of this book.

12. HYBRIDIZING & GROWING FROM SEED

The majority of the plants described in this book are hybrids, many thousands of which have been produced by nurserymen and amateur growers over a period of about 200 years. A hybrid plant is one which arises from the union of two sex cells supplied by genera, species, varieties or cultivars, the sex cells being in the pollen and ovary of the parent plants.

It is generally accepted that a species, if self fertilized, will produce the same species because the genetic material has become stabilized over thousands, perhaps millions of years. Perhaps the form of the progeny will be slightly different, a process which if continuous, will contribute to plant evolution. A hybrid whether cross fertilized or self fertilized can only produce another hybrid as the genetic material of the hybrid has not yet been stabilized over thousands of years.

The process of placing pollen on to the stigma of a plant, the same plant or another is called pollination. If the sex cells unite and form a zygote or fertilized embryo, then fertilization has occurred. If this results in the formation of a seed and this grows, a new hybrid is born. This becomes a new cultivar and may be multiplied by cuttings and if desired given a registered name.

The creation of the first *Pelargonium* hybrid does not seem to be recorded but literature tells us that 700 varieties were available from a London nursery in 1831. Most of these have now faded into limbo, but since then, such is the human desire to create something new, we now have over 15 000 *Pelargonium* cultivar names on record here in Australia. Only a small portion of these are actually available in Australia, or anywhere. There must be an equal or greater number neither given a name nor recorded. This indicates that the creation of new hybrids is a simple and straightforward matter in which all growers may participate and this chapter will give some guidance on procedures. One of the major attributes of *Pelargonium*, over many other plants in the production of hybrids, is the rapid growth rate of the plant and the short interval between seedling and flowering.

Although the serious hybridizer should have a target to aim for, a specific type of plant to produce, perhaps one having a particular type of flower variegation, or leaf shape or disease resistance and so on, the beginner most often has to use whatever plant material is available. For example, pollen is sometimes scarce in small collections and very little may be at hand when the stigma is ripe.

The structure of the *Pelargonium* flower may be seen in the diagrams of Appendix 1. A single flower is shown, as this is typical, but double flowers may be encountered in practice where some of the filaments and stamens have grown as petals. As a result pollen is sometimes scarce in double flowers.

The *Pelargonium* flower is protandrous in that the pollen ripens before the stigma, a natural sequence of events to minimize self fertilization. This means that the female or seed bearing parent will be the flower which is now opening and the male, or pollen bearing plant, will be the flower which is due to open tomorrow or the next day. Pollination is the placing of ripe pollen upon the ripe stigma by any means you care to choose. Some use a fine brush, others a cotton bud, others the anther held in forceps or by dabbing the male flower up against the female flower.

However, before treating this in detail just a word about pollen. This is contained within the anther and when it is ripe the anther splits open along two grooves or sutures. The suture widens and the lips fold out and back exposing the yellow pollen to view. Prior to this the unripe anthers are purple-red or brown-red. Pollen grains are small spherical bodies, those from a zonal measured 70 micrometres in diameter (0.003 inches); those from a regal were a little larger measuring 96 micrometres (0.004 inches). Although each grain is small the pollen mass itself, consisting of hundreds of grains is quite easy to see.

Just after the flower has opened the stigma may be seen as single vertical 'rod' with a slightly rounded tip projecting from the centre of the flower and arising from the ovary. Daily inspection will show that the tip divides into five segments which gradually take up a horizontal position and then commence to curve downwards. When these segments are basically horizontal with a slight downward curve at the tip they are ripe for pollination. If pollination is not done now the arms of the stigma will curve down and it will be too late. Although the line drawings given in this book are helpful, a study of the actual flower parts cannot be bettered, especially if a small magnifying lens is used.

Having selected the seed parent with an inflorescence bearing newly opened flowers, emasculate the flowers by removing the anthers. A pair of forceps is a useful tool for this purpose. It is not always necessary to do this but as it takes only one grain of pollen to fall on the stigma segment to produce a seed, many hybridists like to take this precaution.

The stigma should now be protected from pollination by an insect. If the plant is not in an insect proof enclosure place a paper bag over the inflorescence and tie it loosely around the peduncle. Twice a day remove the bag and inspect the stigma curvature. When it is judged to be ripe remove the pollen from the selected pollen parent and place on to the five stigmatic arms. As not all pollen grains may be live and fertile ensure that each stigmatic arm is covered by at least several grains of pollen. Only one pollen grain will grow down the style from each arm of the stigma and into the ovary but there is usually sufficient pollen to ensure against failure of fertilization.

If a brush is used to convey the pollen ensure that it is washed thoroughly after use to remove any adhering pollen grains, a swirl around in methylated spirits is usually effective. Cotton buds may be discarded after a single usage.

Neither the pollen nor the stigma remain ripe and receptive for very long, perhaps only a day or so, therefore timing is most important. Petals may be removed as these will fall anyway if the action has been successful and there is no longer any need to cover the pollinated flowers. However, there may be other flowers of the inflorescence which were not pollinated so, to avoid confusion, should these subsequently be insect pollinated, remove these or alternatively tie a small label around the pedicel of the flowers to which pollen has been applied. Some growers simply attach a numbered tag to the pedicel as this avoids weighing it down, and record the details against this number in a book. The records should show the name of the pollen parent, the name of the seed parent, the date of pollination, the date of seed collection and the number of seeds obtained. This latter gives some idea of the success rate and the fertility of the cross. The tag may be removed along with the seed and placed in an envelope.

The successful production of seeds will not always ensue, the timing of pollination may have been wrong, perhaps the pollen was not fertile, perhaps the selected parents were not compatible. Experience is a valuable teacher, not only in respect of the above but in the selection of suitable and desirable parents to produce a plant having wanted characteristics. Little seems to be known about this subject, which is not surprising as those who have acquired the knowledge tend to guard this carefully.

Most of the characteristics of a plant are coded into a genetic system carried in the chromosome bodies located in the cell nucleus. Typically identical chromosomes should exist in both the pollen and egg embryo but the genetic codes vary, so allowing the production of plants having minor differences such as petal colour, leaf shape and growth characteristics. However, bodies in the cell other than the nucleus are also responsible for some of the characteristics. This is called cytoplasmic inheritance and is important in that only the seed parent can contribute this to the progeny. The pollen plant is restricted to the supply of nuclear (chromosome) held characteristics. Expressed in another way, pollen A put on to stigma B could well produce a plant quite different to that resulting from pollen B placed on to stigma A.

The plant would be different anyway because as explained previously, the genetic stability of hybrids precludes exact duplication by sexual methods but cytoplasmic inheritance provides yet another possible cause of variation. Whether two plants can be 'crossed' or hybridized depends on their sexual compatibility, primarily the chromosomes of both need to be numerically equal and of the same shape. If this is not so and a cross occurs the progeny may be either monstrosities or something very unusual and also infertile.

A few days after pollination the stigma will dry up and the style and ovary commence to grow. Perhaps the petals may fall off as they now serve no useful purpose. Although this growth occurs it does not mean success, that is, a fertile seed. The pollen carries a plant growth substance (sometimes called a hormone) which swells the ovary and other parts associated with the seed.

The style and ovary will be green and grow to a length of 2 to 3 cms. In time it will go brownish and lose water. When it is dark brown it may be removed from the plant, labelled and stored. For total success there should be five plump seeds in seed cases. Press each seed case between thumb and forefinger, if a hard seed can be felt this is probably fertile. Sometimes the seed case is empty and crushes easily which indicates a failure.

If the seed cases are left on the plant the 'tail' attachment dries out and twists, lifting the seed case away from the style. Heat and dryness also expands the silken 'feather' allowing the wind to whisk the seed case away from the plant. The attachment of the 'tail' is very fragile and breaks off easily and in a hot dry wind it will coil several times in a minute, the movement being quite fast. To avoid loss of seed the point of attachment of the 'tail' may be reinforced by wrapping a small piece of sticky tape around the tip.

Just how long seeds can be kept and still be viable is unknown, many reports say the sooner planting is done the better. Storage in a cool dry place lowers respiration and usage of stored food so must assist longevity. Germination is often rather slow taking some months, other seeds germinate within a few weeks.

Some growers believe, no doubt quite correctly, that germination is faster if the seed is removed from the seed case and the latter discarded. The ventral surface of the seed case, the part up against the style has a suture or groove in it. Insert a needle into this and lever out the seed. It has a tendency to eject rather suddenly and be difficult to find so do this work on a sheet of white paper.

The seed raising mix may vary in its composition but two properties are essential—it must not be soggy and waterlog the seed so as to exclude air and it must remain moist at all times. Drying out of the mix can be fatal for a newly germinated seed. Do not include fertilizers in the mix (unless these are of the slow release type) as the young root is delicate and easily killed by a high salt content of the mix.

A commonly used mix consists of equal parts of fine peat moss and sand or alternatively a sandy loam. Place the seed, or seed case if the seed has not been removed, about 5 mm below the surface of the mix, the tail may be removed if desired. It is advantageous to use one seed per 5 cm pot (thumb pots) for three reasons. This allows easy potting-on without any disturbance to the delicate root system which would set back the growth of the seedling. Digging seedlings out of community pots, punnets or seed flats must surely break or disturb the invisible root hairs of the plant. Secondly seeds which are slow to germinate are not lost or disturbed as they could well be in a seed flat during the removal of seedlings. Lastly, it is much easier to label a single pot unambiguously than it is to label seeds distributed over a seed flat.

Germination is usually accelerated by warmth so try and keep a minimum temperature of 15°C although there is no evidence that this is either optimum or critical. The first indication of germination is the green and bent hypocotyl poking through the surface of the mix (see diagram). This straightens up to display the two cotyledons or seed leaves. The seedling is now able to make its own food substances with the aid of light and some nutrients. At about every third watering add a water soluble fertilizer at no greater than one-quarter normal strength.

The use of pasteurized soil or mix as described in the chapter on *Propagation* is very advantageous for raising seedlings as this minimises disease attack. Try to avoid wetting the soil in the

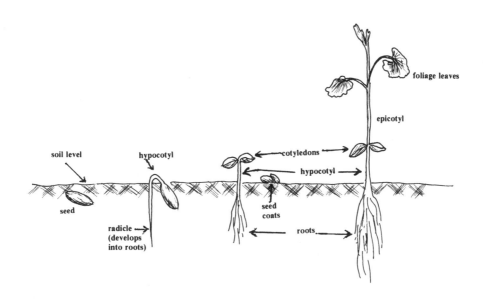

immediate vicinity of the area where the small stem comes through the soil, this is one of the most vulnerable points for fungal attack. If the soil is moist and the seedling shows any sign of wilt cease fertilizer application and flush the pot through with plenty of water.

Before long the true leaves and stem will appear between the cotyledons. Keep the plant in a well lighted place but not in sunshine, carry on with the fertilizer and do not attempt to repot until the seedling has several good size leaves and is 5 to 7 cms high or ever larger.

Future care is now treated in the chapter on *Growing in Containers* even if the plants are ultimately destined to be planted out in the garden.

13. PLANTS FOR EXHIBITION

Beautiful plants grown in containers can be the means of giving pleasure to many people. Beautiful pelargoniums grown in containers of a size that can be easily transported, can not only give pleasure to an even greater number of people, but can be exhibited at shows with other similar plants. Comparisons can be made, new cultivars noted and an awareness of the beauty and variety of the pelargonium can be increased.

Interested readers will find there are geranium and pelargonium societies in many countries of the world (see Appendix 2). Such societies hold shows from time to time and would welcome enquiries.

Competitive showing demands some attention to detail, such as the requirements of a schedule and the 'properties' of a plant for exhibition.

General guide-lines are given below.

1. Check flower show dates with local societies, in gardening magazines or papers.

2. Obtain a copy of the schedule for the show and note carefully the closing date for entries, the time at which plants should be brought to the hall and staged (placed in position on the bench).

3. Read the schedule thoroughly checking the exact class into which plants should be entered. A plant incorrectly entered will be marked N.A.S. (Not According to Schedule), and not judged. Should the schedule appear ambiguous, or contain terms not clearly understood, contact the Show Secretary so that obscurities may be explained.

4. Prepare plants well ahead of show day by keeping them free of disease and insect injury. Containers should be kept clean without trace of mould or dirt. Soil should be kept free of weeds. A light forking on the day of the show, before placing on the bench, adds to the general appearance.

5. Many plants are at their best in their second year, planning should therefore be commenced early by choosing up to six containers of the same type plant. This, because of the variations in rate of development, will ensure that one or two plants are at their prime at the date of the show.

Judges make every effort to be impartial. Preferences for particular colours do not influence their choice, nor do a small number of entries in a class cause them to award a prize just to encourage an exhibitor. Competitive plants are judged to a standard and awarded points for their various attributes.

The process of judging basically consists of two factors; *general* as to the appearance of the exhibit on the show bench, and *specific* as to the plants attributes for point scoring.

General

(a) Plants should be correctly benched (i.e. in the correct class).

(b) Entries should be disease free, with all dead stems, flowers, foliage and stipules removed.

(c) Plant containers should be clean and to the size specified in the schedule. Soil should look fresh and clean and be weed free.

(d) Plants should be well-shaped, rounded and proportionate in size to the container. An aesthetic assessment is approximately one and a half times the height of the container. For instance a tiny miniature in a 25.4 cm (10″) pot would be ludicrous.

(e) Plants should be well foliaged from the base, and showing as growing on one stem only (except in some classes, such as miniatures and some scenteds).

(f) Foliage should be of good colour with clear markings according to the type shown, and free of any powder from recent spraying. A last minute light spray just before benching, with clean water, using an atomiser, will give a fresh clean look. Care should be taken not to allow too much water on the flower petals.

(g) Flower heads (truss, umbel or inflorescence) should be held well clear of the foliage on strong stems, be proportionate in number to the size of the plant, and of a bright, clear and distinct colour. Spent flower heads and individual flowers which are past their prime should be carefully removed before benching (tweezers are ideal for this purpose). Flower buds unopened or just opening should be left on the plant.

(h) The exhibit should be correctly labelled. Clear labelling giving the correct cultivar name is an asset. Should the name be unknown, or the plant a seedling, the label should state this. When the name is unknown it can often be supplied by the judge for the benefit of the exhibitor. Labelling and presentation (in the choice of container used) are usually only taken into consideration when there is a close tie between plants.

Specific

Listed below are the various plant type groups usually included in schedules of geranium and pelargonium societies. The area of emphasis for points in each group, is given first, followed by the more secondary considerations.

FLOWERING PLANTS of zonal, hybrid-zonal, hybrid-ivy, ivy-leaved and regal pelargoniums.

> Flower: Floriferousness (abundance of flowers), size, quality, freshness and colour
> Plant: Shape and culture
> Foliage: Quality and quantity

FANCY-LEAVED PLANTS of zonal, hybrid-ivy, ivy-leaved and regal pelargoniums

> Foliage: Variegation, freshness, clearness and overall consistency of ornamentation
> Plant: Shape and culture
> Flower: Quality, freshness and colour

MINIATURE and MICRO-MINIATURE PLANTS of flowering zonal, ivy-leaved and regal pelargoniums

> Plant: Size, shape and culture
> Flower: Floriferousness, size, quality, freshness and colour
> Foliage: Quality and quantity

MINIATURE and MICRO-MINIATURE PLANTS of fancy-leaved zonal pelargoniums

> Foliage: Variegation, freshness, clearness and overall consistency of ornamentation
> Plant: Size, shape and culture
> Flower: Quality, freshness and colour

SCENTED-LEAVED pelargoniums

> Foliage: Perfume, freshness, quality and quantity
> Plant: Size, shape and culture
> Flower: Quality, quantity, freshness and colour

SCENTED FANCY-LEAVED pelargoniums

> Foliage: Perfume, variegation, freshness, clearness and overall consistency of ornamentation
> Plant: Size, shape and culture
> Flower: Quality, quantity, freshness and colour

SPECIES DERIVED PLANTS such as Unique hybrids and Angel pelargoniums

> Flower: Floriferousness, size, quality, freshness and colour
> Plant: Size, shape and culture
> Foliage: Quality and quantity

SPECIES *Erodium, Geranium* and *Pelargonium* (other than the scented-leaved pelargonium group)

This group requires a specialized judge. Each plant has its own particular type of growth habit, flower form, colour, floriferousness (or otherwise) and season for maximum flowering. The judge should have a knowledge of the genus to which the plant belongs and any characteristics peculiar to that genus.

Competitive plant showing has been a propensity of some gardeners for many years. It is interesting to note that some of the 'Properties' required of geraniums and pelargoniums in the 1800's are equally relevant today.

1.   The petals should be thick, broad, blunt, and smooth at the edges, and slightly cupped.

2.   The flower should be circular, higher at the edges than in the centre (so as to form rather a hollow, though by no means a deeply cupped bloom) without puckering or frilling, and where the petals lap over each other, the indentation caused by the join is hardly perceptible.

3.   The petals should lie close on each other, so as to appear a whole flower rather than a five-petalled flower.

4.   The stem should be straight, strong, elastic, carrying the blooms well above the foliage. The footstalks of the individual flowers should be stiff, and of sufficient length to allow the flowers to show themselves in an even head, fitting compactly edge to edge, and forming a uniform bold truss.

5.   The colour should be bright and dense, whether it be scarlet, crimson, rose-colour, boldly contrasted with the ground, and the darker the better, both upper petals should be alike, both side petals alike, and the lower petal uniform.

6.   All white grounds should be very pure, and the colours, no matter what they be, on the white,

should be decided, well defined and by no means flush into the white.

7.   The spots on the upper petals, or the marks in any other, should not break through to the edge.

8.   Colours being a matter of taste, do not affect the real properties so much as other points, unless it be on the score of novelty, on this ground a bright scarlet would be desirable, and a black spot. We have plenty of approaches to both, but none very near.

9.   The plant should be shrubby in its habit, the foliage close, and of a rich bright green, the joints short and strong, able to support themselves in every part without assistance. The flower should be large, not less than five in a truss, and come at the end of every shoot.

The obvious faults of most geraniums are, long and pointed lower petals, uneven, twisted, notched or puckered edges, long footstalks, which make the truss loose and open, weak shoots and stalks that will not hold up the flowers without propping, which destroys the appearance of the plant altogether, small leaves and long joints, which make the plant open, the habit gawky and the foliage poor.

The great object of the cultivator for exhibition, according to the present fashion, should be strength, bushy habit, quantity of bloom and colour of foliage. This is not to be accomplished by exciting composts for rapid growth induces long instead of short joints and nothing goes further towards spoiling habit.

Gardeners, like other sections of the population, vary in their competitive spirit but for those that have it, they will find that growing plants for exhibition not only improves their knowledge of the family and their prowess as gardeners, but brings pleasure and interest to the public.

14. PESTS, PATHOGENS & PROBLEMS

This chapter is included to aid pelargonium growers in recognizing the pests and pathogenic diseases which are likely to cause trouble and other problems which may occur. Although the list is fairly long, not all pelargoniums are susceptible to all those listed and, of course, a pest, pathogen or problem which may be rampant in one part of Australia (or even in one garden) may be missing elsewhere.

As with all potential problems, 'prevention is better than cure'. To neglect a perceived problem may be fatal: it is therefore wise to inspect plants regularly for signs of trouble to enable problems to be 'nipped in the bud'. As mentioned in the chapter on *Pruning & Shaping*, it is always wise to grow on a couple of cuttings of your favourites as insurance against loss. Pelargoniums are soft and make succulent hosts for predators, fungal spores, bacteria and viruses: once taken hold, the plant will die quickly. In this event, the plant is best discarded immediately (preferably burnt in an incinerator) so that it is not a source of infection for the rest of your collection.

As with other plants, a healthy, well-grown and maintained pelargonium is more likely to be able to resist pest and disease attack than a poor neglected specimen. Therefore good cultural practices prove an invaluable aid as defence against possible problems.

The following list of pests and diseases is not meant to be exhaustive; rather, the pathogens included are those considered most likely to attack pelargoniums at some time or another.

PESTS

Caterpillars. Many species of caterpillars attack pelargoniums causing two types of damage: chewing around the edge of leaves and creating holes in leaves, and tunnelling into flower buds. Some species cocoon themselves inside a rolled up leaf. Most of this damage occurs at night during the spring and summer months. It is a good idea to start spraying when moths and/or butterflies are noticed hovering over the plants and then as soon as the larvae emerge from the eggs, they eat already sprayed surfaces. The eggs may be seen as tiny dark pinpricks. However, it is not always possible to be this vigilant and when first noticed, the damage may be considerable—a small plant with half a dozen leaves can be denuded overnight. The presence of caterpillars may be signalled by their droppings on the leaf surfaces—the place to look for caterpillars is on the *underside* of the leaf *above*. They are usually to be found lying parallel to the main vein. Caterpillars attacking flower buds are usually seen poking out of the hole they have bored into the bud. Very tiny caterpillars are also found tucked right into the bottom of the inflorescence where the pedicels join the peduncle (see Appendix 1).

The most obvious control is to pick off by hand; however, for continuing protection spray with Dipel every seven to ten days, on both surfaces of leaves as well as flower buds. Dipel is especially formulated for caterpillars and is harmless to all other pests and animals. However, it takes two or three days to have any effect as the caterpillars must ingest the sprayed surfaces. For a more immediate kill, a pyrethrum-based pressure-pak may be used, or for a severe infestation, a pesticide containing the active ingredient carbaryl may be used. This is a toxic substance and must therefore be handled with appropriate care. (Both Dipel and/or a carbaryl-based powder may be mixed with Zineb for the control of rust on zonals. However, for compatibility of other sprays, refer to directions on the respective packets.)

White Fly (also known as Greenhouse White Fly). This pest mainly attacks regal and scented-leaved pelargoniums but can be a pest of zonals as well. White Flies suck sap causing leaves to turn yellow and drop. The adult white fly is about 1 mm in length with white wings covered in a waxy powder. They are usually detectable because they fly out in a cloud when the plant is disturbed. An examination of the undersides of the leaves will reveal the eggs which have been laid. With four nymphal stages, the life cycle takes approximately 30 days to complete. However, as the hatching of the eggs may overlap, it is necessary to spray once a week for a month or more to eradicate completely. If there are only a few white flies present, with a certain amount of deftness, these may be squashed by hand. The eggs may be wiped off the back of the leaves with a soapy cloth. However, this is tedious and the leaves are easily damaged. Alternatively, spray the underside of the leaves with Malathion or a pyrethrum-based insecticide. If using pyrethrum, several sprayings may be required as this is a very quick-acting insecticide with a very short (maybe only half an hour) residual period. Malathion should be used allowing seven to ten days between applications, two or three sprayings often being necessary to kill successive generations of the insect.

White flies exude a sweet sticky substance called honeydew and on this honeydew a fungus called black sooty mould forms. This is unsightly but will disappear eventually if treatment for white fly is carried out. Ants may also be present in search of the honeydew.

Aphids. Aphids are insects about 1 mm in length, with fat, rounded, soft bodies. They are of various colours, green being the most common on pelargoniums. They suck sap and are found in clusters around flower buds and new shoots. A severe infestation may cause leaves to dry and curl and distortion of buds and flowers. A few aphids, noticed early, may be rubbed off by hand; otherwise spray with a pyrethrum-based product or Malathion. Aphids also excrete honeydew. A cultural control for minimizing aphid attack is to keep plants well watered in dry seasons: dry plants have a concentrated sap which is very nourishing to aphids.

Mealy Bugs. Little blobs of what looks like cottonwool clustered in the leaf axils, along midribs of leaves and around flower buds denote the presence of mealy bugs. The white substance is a powdery wax which covers a body more likely to be yellow, pink or a purply-grey colour. Around the body is a fringe of wax threads with two long filaments at the back. They may be up to 5 mm in length and are sap-suckers eventually causing the plant to wilt. As mealy bugs are easily detectable and recognizable, early eradication is a fairly simple procedure. They may be rubbed off by hand, but this is a sticky business and it may also be difficult to remove them from between the pedicels of the flowers without breaking these somewhat brittle stems. Alternatively, a dab with a cotton bud dipped in methylated spirits is most effective. For a heavy infestation, spray with Malathion plus White Oil.

Soil Mealy Bugs. These pests suck sap from roots. They are found beneath soil level (in pots, usually near the edge of the inside of the pot—clusters of eggs may also be seen at bottom of pots). These mealy bugs are approximately 1 mm in length with thin bodies and covered in a white waxy substance. Above ground symptoms are lack of growth and few flowers. To eradicate, drench the soil with a Malathion solution (4 mls to 1 litre water)—this should be repeated twice at seven to ten day intervals to kill successive generations of the insect. Alternatively, if in a pot and the plant seems beyond recovery, it should be burned and the soil drenched in boiling water or pasteurized in an oven at 60°C (140°F) for 30 minutes.

Perhaps less common among *Pelargonium* pests are spider mites and nematodes.

Spider Mites may be a problem in extended periods of dry weather. The adults are extremely tiny and appear as black dots on the underside of leaves. Their sap-sucking causes foliage to take on a mottled or bleached appearance. A heavy infestation results in fine silken webbing covering the plant. Kelthane insecticide is especially formulated for mites and should be used if possible; otherwise Rogor may be substituted. An alternative control is to use Disyston granules sprinkled on the soil and watered in—use according to directions on the pack.

Nematodes (also known as eelworms) are tiny worm-like, almost transparent, parasites approximately 1 mm in length which live in the soil. They favour sandy conditions and cause damage by attacking the root system—roots may become knotted, form galls, branch excessively or have injured tips, their function being severely decreased. Nematodes may also facilitate the introduction of fungi, bacteria and viruses into the plant. Above ground manifestation of the presence of nematodes is revealed by slowing of growth, yellowing of foliage, excessive and rapid wilting in hot or dry weather. If a plant is found to be thus affected, it is best destroyed (cuttings may be taken if it is not too far gone) and the soil treated at 60°C (140°F) for 30 minutes. Alternatively, drench the soil with products especially formulated for nematode control such as Nemacur or Nemagon. To combat further infestations, introduce more organic matter into the soil, this facilitates predatory nematodes and fungi to keep populations of pathogenic and root-attacking nematodes in check.

PATHOGENIC DISEASES

Fungi which attack plants are microscopic organisms which spread and grow by long threads of living tissue. This usually commences to grow from a spore lodged on the external surface of the plant and penetrates into the plant through a natural opening or by softening the plant tissue and so entering to absorb its food supply from the plant. Spores are produced by the mature parts of the fungus, are microscopic in size and spread by wind or simply fall on to healthy plant tissue. These are virtually the 'seeds' of the fungus. Fungicides act by being present on the plant tissue at the time the spore germinates and kill the newly emerged thread (hypha). The spore is then exhausted and can do no further harm. Only systemic fungicides can kill a fungus once it is inside the plant.

Rust (*Puccinia pelargonii-zonalis*) (see **Plate 98**). A common disease of zonal pelargoniums and well known to most growers, rust appears as concentric circles of rust-coloured pustules on the underside of leaves. On the upper leaf surface there are corresponding green spots. As the infestation spreads the leaves turn yellow but the affected areas remain green. The fungal spores are spread by wind and splashing of water, particularly in hot humid weather. If plants have sufficient air circulation and are inspected regularly, the disease can be easily kept under control. At the first sign of rust, the affected leaves should be removed and destroyed (preferably burnt). If there are several affected plants scattered about the garden, it is best to carry a paper bag around and drop the 'rusty' leaves into this as soon as they are picked off the plant—this avoids spreading the spores. Plants may then be sprayed with Plantvax or Zineb, making sure both surfaces of the leaves are thoroughly covered. An aid in adhering the fungicide to leaf surfaces is a drop of detergent in the mixture (one drop per half a litre of mixture). Excess application of nitrogenous fertilizer should be avoided.

Black Stem Rot. Caused by the fungus *Pythium splendens*, black stem rot takes its name from the black appearance and subsequent rotting of the stem. The disease starts at the bottom of the stem and rapidly spread upwards. It may sometimes be confused with bacterial stem rot (see below) but is distinguished by the fact that the topmost leaves on the plant fold inwards or 'cup'. The petioles may also bend upwards. As the disease travels up the stem, the petioles fall off, thus defoliating the plant. The optimum temperature for *Pythium* growth is 30°C. It is spread by contaminated soil, splashing water and excessive soil moisture. Cuttings as well as mature plants can be affected. Once the plant or cutting has developed black stem rot, it is beyond hope and should be destroyed immediately. To aid in prevention of the disease, use pasteurized media for cuttings and dip cuttings in a fungicide or use a fungicide soil drench (as described in the chapter on *Propagation by Cutting*). Mature plants in the ground should be pulled out and burned and the soil drenched with a 10% Formalin solution. (If the area is surrounded by other plants, these may be adversely affected by Formalin.) Allow at least a week before replanting in the same spot and during this time fork the soil over to aerate it.

Leaf Spot (*Cercospora brunkii*) is recognized as small, light brown spots on the leaves that become darker and larger with age. As the disease progresses the spots merge, the leaf tissue between them turning yellow. Leaf margins may become ragged and the leaves show curling or twisting. Overcrowding of plants encourages this fungal disease, as does evening watering which increases humidity, thus creating conditions for the disease to flourish. Control by removing all infected leaves and spraying plant with a fungicide containing copper oxychloride. (Spraying with fungicides is a preventive measure and will not 'cure' those parts of the plant already affected.)

Grey Mould *(Botrytis cinerea).* This fungus first appears on dead areas of flowers, stems or leaves and develops into a grey downy growth. It flourishes in cool humid weather and is spread by wind-blown spores. The prompt removal of dead parts of the plant will aid in the prevention of this disease. Dead leaves and flowers that have fallen from the plant should also be removed to deprive the fungus of dead tissue to grow on. This should be done as carefully as possible to avoid spreading the spores. Evening watering should be avoided and plants should have adequate air circulation and sunlight. Bordeaux, Benlate or Dacomil may be sprayed to control grey mould.

Verticillium Wilt. A disease attacking zonals and regals, this fungus causes the leaves to wilt, starting in the middle or upper portion of the main stem or side branches. The onset of this disease is very rapid and can occur virtually overnight. Leaves turn yellow and the petiole also wilts. Eventually the whole plant becomes affected, the leaves fall and parts of the stem may blacken, with resultant death. The disease is spread by infected cuttings and soil. Affected plants should be destroyed and soil treated with Formalin solution as described above for black stem rot.

BACTERIA

Bacteria are microscopic organisms, a few of which attack plants, some producing powerful toxins which eventually kill the plant tissue. Unlike fungi, each bacterium is an individual and does not produce long infective threads. They live in moist conditions, only and must normally penetrate the plant rapidly, through natural openings, or die. Bacteria are transferred from an infected plant to another by infected cutting tools or by water droplets splashed around, especially those splashed up from soil. Once inside the plant stem there is little that can be done although infected leaves may be removed.

Bacterial Leaf Spot and Stem Rot (see **Plate 97** for bacterial leaf spot). The bacterium *Xanthomonas pelargonii* first appears as pinhead-sized spots on the leaves, developing into irregular watery brown and sunken blotches. This bacterium also occurs as a darkening of the stem tip, spreading downwards or may start at the base of the stem and work upwards. It differs from the fungus *Pythium splendens* in that the leaves start to droop around the margin, the petiole remains straight but falls downwards and as the disease progresses, falls off the plant. The bacteria enter the plant through wounds or the stomates in the leaves and are spread by splashing water (thereby transferring the bacteria from infected soil onto the plant) and overcrowding of plants. Infected tops of stems may be pruned off at least 50 mm below the darkened area. Plants with basal stem rot should be removed and burned—soil should be treated as detailed for control of *Pythium*, above.

VIRUSES

At the present time there is no known cure for viral diseases. The problem is overcome in the nursery trade by growing new plants from virus-free stock and by using the meristem (growing tip) from which to propagate. (Other texts may be consulted for details of meristem culture.) Viruses do not cause plants to die (indeed, the markings on foliage or flowers are often considered attractive and plants known to contain viruses are deliberately propagated to maintain the markings; for further details, see below). However, in some cases, viruses may cause leaves to become distorted, flowers to abort and the spotting of folliage. Viruses may also reduce the overall vigour of the plant. The condition is spread by the use of infected tools and insect attack such as aphids and nematodes. The most commonly recognized symptoms of viruses are as follows:

Chlorosis—yellow spotting on leaves (see **Plate 94**).

Crinkle or Leaf Curl—spots that yellow with age, turn brown and expand causing distortion of leaves. This virus is transmitted by the pelargonium aphid, *Macrosiphum pelargonii.*

Mosaic—disappearance of leaf zonation and purple spotting along veins.

Yellow Net Venation—as mentioned above, this is one manifestation of the presence of a virus considered attractive and perpetuated in the *Pelargonium* genus by taking cuttings from infected plants. A popular example is the ivy-leaved cultivar 'White Mesh' (see illustration of this plant in colour plates). The particular virus concerned causes the veins of leaves to turn pale yellow.

Greening Virus—small green flowers appear instead of the normal colour.

Unwanted virus-infected plants should be removed and burned—soil treatment as for *Pythium*, above.

PROBLEMS

Oedema (also Edema). This comes under the heading of 'Problem' (as opposed to Pests or Pathogens) and may develop when the soil is warm and moist and the air cool and moist. It appears as tiny pimple-like blisters on the undersides of leaves and on petioles and stems. These enlarge and turn brown and corky. Affected leaves yellow and drop off. The condition is a physiological one whereby the plant is taking in more moisture than it can give off (via transpiration), thus causing the cells to burst. It can be overcome by spacing plants to allow for good air circulation and by not overwatering during periods of cloudy cool weather.

It will be observed that several pests, pathogens and problems exhibit similar symptoms and call for similar control measures. As mentioned above, sprays for some pests and diseases may be mixed (if compatible) to enable preventive maintenance for a number of problems to be carried out concurrently. With regular tours of inspection and a prompt response to perceived problems, many of the above-listed pests and diseases may be avoided.

Nutrient Deficiencies. Sometimes plants suffer from a deficiency of a nutrient. This causes various symptoms to appear on the leaf and permits diagnosis of the problem. However, this requires some practice as these symptoms may be confused with those caused by diseases or other cultural conditions.

Additionally, one must be very familiar with the normal growth habit of the plant in question. Perhaps that yellowing around the edge of the leaf is a genetic feature of that particular cultivar; many pelargoniums are naturally stunted; many have leaves that tend to cup or twist; and so on.

The diagnosis of deficiencies should therefore be approached with caution. It should also be pointed out that a certain amount of leaf yellowing and leaf fall will occur in the natural life of the plant. Pelargoniums are mostly quick growers and lose leaves fairly rapidly, particularly during late summer and autumn as they approach the end of their main flowering period.

It should also be emphasized that a diagnosis should not be based on the examination of only one leaf: the appearance and growth habit of the entire plant should be taken into consideration.

Deficiencies in one or more nutrients may be caused by: its absence from the potting mix, either in the original mix or because of its exhaustion by the plant and micro-organisms in the mix; or it is in plentiful supply but is unavailable to the plant for various reasons, as, for example, incorrect pH value of the mix or because it is bound up with other substances in the mix, vermiculite for example, or because it has been converted to an insoluble form.

Although all nutrient elements cause the plant to exhibit deficiency symptoms, only five will be listed here as the most common or likely. These are nitrogen (nitrates or ammonium), phosphorus, potassium, magnesium and iron.

The major diagnostic characteristic is whether either the older leaves or new leaves are symptomatic. Some nutrients are very mobile within the plant and when the supply from the roots is limited, leave the older growth to supply the new growth. Others are not mobile within the plant and when a limited supply occurs the young leaves exhibit the deficiency.

NITROGEN

Diagnosis: Older leaves mostly affected. Plant light green, lower leaves turn yellow and dry to a light brown colour.
Remedy: Apply fertilizer containing nitrates, ammonium compounds or urea. These are all very soluble and should be applied in water at a rate no greater than stated on the packet.

PHOSPHORUS

Diagnosis: Older leaves mostly affected. Plant dark green, often developing red-purple colours, lower leaves may be yellow and dry off to a blue-green colour and fall.
Remedy: Apply phosphatic fertilizer preferably a water soluble one such as ammonium phosphate (usually contained in commercial water soluble fertilizers). Only small quantities of phosphate fertilizer are required but a deficiency is catastrophic. Superphosphate may be applied and forked in. However, it is not very soluble and is best used for long term correction.

POTASSIUM

Diagnosis: Older leaves mostly affected. Leaves mottled, usually with small spots of dead tissue. Leaves may appear greyish green. In advanced state leaves develop marginal scorching.
Remedy: Apply chloride of potash or sulphate of potash. These are highly soluble so use sparingly—half a teaspoon to a 10 cm pot being sufficient—to obtain correction.

MAGNESIUM

Diagnosis: Older leaves mostly affected. Mottling of leaves but no drying up evident. Yellowing between veins with veins remaining green.
Remedy: Apply a small amount of Epsom salts (magnesium sulphate) to the pot—this is very soluble, so ¼ teaspoon to a 10 cm pot should be sufficient. For long term correction, apply dolomite at the rate of two level teaspoons to 10 cm pot and fork in. If garden lime has been used in the potting mix it is not advisable to add the dolomite until the pH has been checked otherwise soil may become too alkaline and produce other problems.

IRON

Diagnosis: Only newer leaves are affected. They yellow between the veins which remain green—symptoms similar to Magnesium deficiency in appearance.
Remedy: Apply iron chelates to surface of mix and fork in. These are very soluble so use sparingly at about ⅛ teaspoon to a 10 cm pot. Iron is not required in large quantities and is unlikely to be a problem when soil is used in the potting mix. In a soil-less potting mix, however, it may show up as a deficiency.

In the foregoing emphasis has been placed on the small quantities of soluble fertilizers which should be used. The tendency is to think that correction of a shortage requires heaps of the deficient substance. This is not so and can be harmful as a sudden influx of a water soluble fertilizer will cause the roots to lose water and die which then causes further problems.

If plants are given a *light*, regular and frequent (say, once a fortnight) feeding with a balanced fertilizer containing all the essential macro and micro nutrients, none of the above symptoms should appear. Correction procedures to supply one particular nutrient are usually only necessary in cases where soil being used for a potting mix is known to be deficient in that nutrient (for example most Australian soils are low in phosphate).

15. MUTATIONS, SPORTS & REVERSIONS

Pelargoniums, like many other plants, have a tendency to produce deviations from the normal and established flower, leaf or plant form. Such deviations are called "mutations", "sports" or "reversions". These three terms are often not clearly understood and therefore misused so perhaps some simple definitions will help to avoid confusion.

A "sport" is a shoot or part of a plant differing markedly from the typical characteristics of the plant on which it has appeared. Such variation is caused by a "mutation" which is a change in the genetic make up of an organism such as a plant, and resulting from new combinations of genes and chromosomes. Such internal changes, known as mutations may be caused spontaneously, by the planned use of radiation, or by a virus infection.

The external application of chemicals to a plant may cause a deviation from its normal appearance; for example dwarfing, but this is not a mutation unless such deviation is due to a change in its genetic make up. So the dividing line between a mutation and a simple chemical inhibition is not always clear from observation of a change in a plant's appearance.

A "reversion" occurs when a hybrid plant having been in cultivation for some time, suddenly shows the characteristics of one of its parents, or of previous parents. The whole plant, or any other part of the plant such as the flower or leaf may suddenly revert. In the case of a partial reversion such material should be removed to prevent total reversion. The tendency to revert to the ancestral type makes a reversion less desirable than a sport. Whilst the number of cultivars introduced from such reversions is small, many good plants have been developed by careful selection of variations resulting from sports. More are continually being found, selected and introduced.

Plants which have been hybridized to a great extent are not stable genetically. When new tissue is being formed the constituent cells are being multiplied. This requires that new chromosomes also be produced from the chromosomes existing in the original cells. This is done by a replication process using an existing half chromosome as the pattern and building up a new mirror image of it alongside, for use by the new cell. This is a most complex process and the wonder of it all is that the process is so often successful. However, errors do occur in the process and different gene characters are formed. These changes are in turn replicated into the next cell, to the next one after that, and so on some millions of times. This change is seen as leaf colouration, change in flower colour and in other ways, and this piece of changed tissue is called a sport. If the leaves have chlorophyll (i.e. they have some green in them) the piece of tissue can be removed from the parent plant when it is large enough and grown on. If after about three years it is still stable in its characteristics it may be treated as a new cultivar and named.

Sometimes sports appearing as deformities or monstrosities (teratological forms) are produced and naturally these are not worth growing. However the many good sports introduced over the years, and still being produced, are worthy of attention.

The following is a sample list of some that are presently available.

Zonal pelargoniums	a sport from	Zonal pelargoniums	a sport from
'New Life'	'Vesuvius'	'Fiat' ('Pink Fiat')	'Gorgeous'
'Phlox New Life'	'New Life'	'Fiat Queen'	'Pink Fiat'
'Double New Life'	'Wonderful'	'Fiat King'	'Fiat Queen'
'Salmon Vesuvius'	'Vesuvius'	'Princess Fiat'	'Fiat Queen'
'White Vesuvius'	'Vesuvius'	'Royal Fiat'	'Princess Fiat'
'Red Black Vesuvius'	'Vesuvius'		

In the above list of sports, a short one taken at random, it is interesting to note the tendency of some groups of cultivars to sport a line of variations. Many of the plants listed have produced varying forms of ornamentation in the leaves, others, differing flower colours and shapes such as in the 'Fiat' group.

These have all been brought about over the years, by some discerning gardener noticing such variation and taking the trouble to grow the sport until stable, and subsequently introduce it.

By "mutation" nature provides the opportunity for observant gardeners to add to the list of "sports".

APPENDIX 1: ANATOMY OF THE PLANT

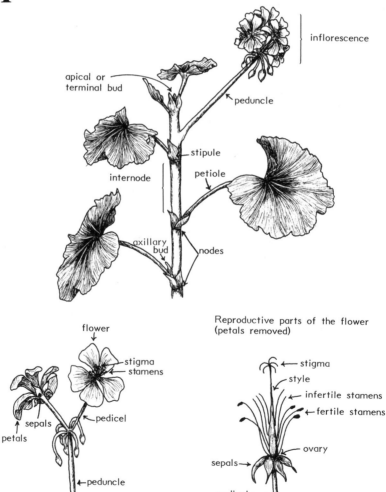

APPENDIX 2: LIST OF SOCIETIES

Australian Geranium Society,
The Science Centre,
35-43 Clarence Street,
SYDNEY NSW 2000

Australian Geranium Society,
Queensland Division,
Naranga Avenue,
Florida Gardens,
SURFERS PARADISE Queensland 4117

Australian Pelargonium and
Geranium Society,
10 Porter Street,
TEMPLESTOWE Victoria 3106

Canberra Geranium and Fuchsia Society,
5 Savage Street,
CAMPBELL ACT 2601

South Australian Geranium and
Pelargonium Society Inc.,
44 Young Street,
UNLEY South Australia 5061

West Australian Geranium Society,
5 Kirwan Street,
FLOREAT West Australia 6014

Canada

Canadian Geranium and
Pelargonium Society,
4124 Hoskins Road,
NORTH VANCOUVER BC V7K 2P5

United Kingdom

The British and European
Geranium Society,
"Morval" The Hills,
BRADWELL Sheffield S30 2HZ

The British Pelargonium and
Geranium Society,
1 Mayfield Close,
Badshot Lea Road,
Badshot Lea,
FARNHAM Surrey GU9 9NJ

Western Counties Pelargonium and
Geranium Society,
Flat 3, 29 Castle Road,
CLEVEDON Avon BS21 7DA

Republic of South Africa

South African Pelargonium and
Geranium Society,
P.O. Box 55342,
Northlands,
JOHANNESBURG 2116

The Netherlands

Nederlandse Pelargonium en
Geranium Vereniging,
Hollands End 89,
1244 NP Ankeveen

United States of America

International Geranium Society,
6501 Yosemite Drive,
BUENA PARK California 90620

San Diego Geranium Society,
Casa del Prade,
BALBOA PARK SAN DIEGO
California 92101

INDEX OF PLANT NAMES

(Page numbers are in roman, plate numbers are in bold type)